Oct. 27, 2012

Spiritual Treasures of
Downtown San Antonio

To Vic & Mary T.

Blessings,

Mary Jane Hardy

©2012 Mary Jane Hardy

Book and cover design by Fishead Design Studio
www.fisheadproductions.com

Printing by Litho Press, Inc.
www.lithopress.net
ISBN 978-0-615-69030-8

Published in the United States of America

Spiritual Treasures of Downtown San Antonio

Mary Jane Hardy

DEDICATION

To my faithful friend and husband

Kenneth A. Hardy

and to my children Dianne, Kristina, and Kenneth II,

and to my grandchildren Emily, Mark, Raquel, and Tina

ACKNOWLEDGEMENTS

Writing this book was a challenge for me. However, it also brought me great pleasure. I learned so much and met so many fascinating and good people. I am sincerely and deeply grateful to all who helped me on this literary journey. The late John W. O'Shea, M.D., was my first and loyal supporter. Brother Edward Loch, S.M., Archivist of the Archdiocese of San Antonio, shared his vast knowledge of local church history. Sister Margaret Patrice Stattery, CCVI, Past President of Incarnate Word College, edited, guided, and gently encouraged me in every aspect of my work. Stewart Allen, research physicist, patiently photographed churches in the sweltering summer heat. My daughter, Dianne Hardy, MSSW, opened my eyes to the joys and excitement of research. Theresa Gold, historian, aided me with her extensive expertise in Texas history. A kind English teacher, Milinda Schwab, proofread the book. Charles A. John, ALA, assisted me in the architectural aspects of churches.

I am thankful also for the many friends who listened, shared laughter, and offered their support: Archbishop Jose H. Gomez, STD, Msgr. Lawrence Steubben, Father Bill Davis, OMI, Father John J. Gordon, OMI, Father Quang D. Van, Father Joseph Mary Marshall, S.M., Father Virgilio Elizondo, Father David Garcia, the late Father Ignacio A. Blanco, C.M.F., Father Paschal C. Amagba, C.M.F., Sister Rosemary Meiman, O.S.U., Kristina Voelkel, Gary Voelkel, Ken Hardy II, Phyllis Allen, Craig Johnson, Jur Van Hoorn, Chrystal Ginder, Mary Gohary, Bob Greer, Jane Greer, Maureen O'Shea, Pat Maguire, Ann Voelkel, Pat Voelkel, Jo Neesvig, Marian Greer, Chad Haddock, Lee Loving, Kay Kutchins, Cleo Edmund, Doran Dennis, David W. Shulman, MD, Pat Hutchison Noble, Cristina Slaughter, Cathy Ruffo Aguirre, Gloria Ferruzzi, Rose Marie Pagonis, Frank Pantuso, Sam Greco, Forrest Fitzhugh, Richard Erickson, Adela Gott, Jeanne Berkheisier, Mary Renteria, Betty Briggs, Polly Atkinson, Ruth (Buttercup) Sparks, Barbara Petit, Diane Sartor, Maxine Balistreri, Ria Spetzler, Hartmut Spetzler, Shirley Hutzler, Nancy Dugger, John Walsh, Betty Curry, Esther Cruz, Albert Cruz, Alice Reyes, Rosemary Brevard, Christie Ethington, Kristina Mondragon, and Barbara Olivares.

I want to express my appreciation also to the many strangers I met as I traveled from church to church, who supported me by giving me free parking places, kind words, and smiles as they learned about my project.

Lastly, I must confess that at times I felt like giving up, but the spirit of my husband, Ken Hardy, seemed to urge me to keep telling people about the spiritual treasures of San Antonio.

TABLE OF CONTENTS

INTRODUCTION

The old majestic churches of downtown San Antonio have been a lifelong fascination of mine. I first became enamored of them while riding the bus from my Southside home to St. Mary's School in the center of the city. As a twelve-year-old girl, I reveled in the chance to explore the area. Every day, as the bus left me on the corner of Navarro Street and Houston Street, I walked from Walgreen's Drugstore past the grand department stores of Frost Bros., Vogue, and Carl's, as well as the Majestic Theatre. Intertwined among these large buildings and busy streets were several beautiful churches that always caught my eye with their high steeples, chiming bells, and luminescent stained glass windows.

I was familiar with some of the Catholic churches, such as St. Mary's. Attending daily Mass at this magnificent church touched my heart and soul. I was captivated by the splendor and size of the incredible structure and simply loved it. Other churches in the area, however, belonged to different religious denominations that I knew nothing about but was always curious to understand their backgrounds, to appreciate their structures, and to know more about their congregations.

A few years later, on my way back and forth to Providence High school, I walked down St. Mary's Street and waited for the bus by the famous Hertzberg clock. During the walk, I was exposed to even more places of worship. Four years later, I was on my way to Incarnate Word College, still taking the bus to class every day and still admiring the striking churches, wondering how they were built, what they looked like inside, who the founders were, and who were the people who gathered there to pray.

I always enjoyed studying history, and when I later became a teacher, my growing understanding of the past of San Antonio gave me new insight into the significance of these beautiful downtown structures. I came to realize how important they were to the formation of the city itself. While many people are familiar with the vital role San Fernando Church, now a cathedral, played in the early days of San Antonio, they are not aware that other historic churches, both Protestant and Catholic, also had significant influence on the development and creation of the city as we know it today.

When I married my beloved husband, Ken Hardy, our growing family and my work as a teacher took me away from regularly visiting the downtown area. Like so many San Antonians of this era, Ken and I attended church in the burgeoning suburban districts where we now lived, but the vivid memories of those historic churches in downtown San Antonio remained with me.

Life would eventually call me back to these magnificent buildings. One day, as my husband was having a serious operation at the Metropolitan Methodist Hospital, I took my now adult children to both St. Mary's Church and St. Joseph's Church to pray for his recovery. I was deeply affected by the spiritual comfort and inspiration I felt during this difficult time, and I was surprised that my children who had never visited the churches before were inspired by the majesty of these places. I realized then that I had not shared this part of my life with them and I regretted this omission. They were growing up in a city rich in history and spirituality yet had missed the opportunity to enjoy the historic and spiritual wonders of downtown San Antonio. If this void existed in the lives of my own children, I was sure it could be found in the lives of many others who knew only the sprawling suburbs of the city.

When my husband recovered from his surgery, we were determined to explore the historic churches in a more in-depth way and to share this rich heritage with our family. We actually went inside each of the downtown churches and became deeply impressed with both the Protestant and Catholic congregations and the many ways they had contributed to the development of San Antonio. We came to know first-hand the invaluable spiritual guidance they had provided to hundreds of thousands of people just like ourselves. We also felt a need to tell the stories of these spiritual treasures so that they might be passed on to future generations.

This book is an attempt to share information on the mission and history of these churches, to describe briefly their architectural designs, and to provide a few stories of human interest associated with each congregation. Part of this work Ken and I researched together, but after his death in 2008, I realized I would have to complete the book alone. Visiting and learning about each one of the churches as I struggled with grief over my husband's death and my own recovery from breast cancer provided me with an unbelievable spiritual power. I had never experienced a feeling like this before, and I believe it provided me with the emotional strength and passion I needed to complete the work.

Although there are many magnificent churches and denominations in other areas of San Antonio, my study is limited to those constructed in the downtown area in the very early years, 1719-1927. I sincerely hope the information contained herein will serve as a guidebook and encourage other persons to enjoy and visit these churches and to become aware of the historic and spiritual beauty they offer.

Mary Jane Hardy

[Our Catholic faith and attending parish services were of such great importance to both my husband Ken and myself that during our early marriage we specifically purchased our first home because of its location adjacent to Holy Spirit Catholic Church, which we wanted to be an integral part of our lives. Our children went to Mass every Sunday with us, and each vacation, the first thing my husband did was to find a church for Mass. This custom did not always delight our children yet it seemed to have had a deep effect on them that is expressed in the poem printed below. It was written by my daughter, Dianne, when she was a fifteen-year-old student at Ursuline Academy in San Antonio. Her English teacher asked her to submit it for publication in a religious magazine, but she never did so. I found it when I was writing this book. It seemed to fit well into the goal of my venture, and I am proud to share it with you my reader.]

PART OF HISTORY . . .

"It is so big."

"I think that is why people always whisper in church; its size makes us realize how small we really are."

"It is so beautiful. Who built it?"

"I think some cloistered monks in about 1700. Can you imagine what that kind of life would have been like?"

"You know, I think that is what attracts me most to the church. Think about all those people who dedicated their lives to this. I can't dedicate myself to an hour of homework. Can you imagine giving a lifetime?"

"All those stories! We've heard them since we were little, but have you ever really listened to them? They are beautiful. Sometimes I start thinking about all the people who've heard those stories. What did they feel? Did they feel like me? There must be a million stories."

"There are probably a million stories in here alone."

"You're right. Look at all those candles. I wonder who they are lit for."

"Maybe a mother lit one for her lost son."

"A child for her grandfather . . . "

"A friend for another . . ."

"I wonder who lit the first one."

"Look at the cross. I wonder who carved it. Maybe it was some old carpenter who was so honored to make it that he didn't accept a penny for it."

"Maybe it was a young man who charged as much as he could get."

"I wonder who said the first Mass."

"How many people knelt here?"

"Can you imagine how many prayers have been said here? Millions . . ."

Silence.

"I kinda feel overwhelmed."

"I feel small."

"There is so much history here. We'll never know any of it. You want to go?"

"Yeah, just a minute – I'm going to light a candle. I want to be part of history."

Dianne Hardy
1981

TIMELINE

- Indigenous people lived in the area of Texas for over 11,000 to 40,000 years before historians began to record significant dates and events.

- **1519**   Alonso Alvarez de Pineda maps the Texas coastline, setting boundaries for the state.

- **1528**   Cabeza de Vaca investigates the interior of Texas.

- **1540**   Francisco Vasquez de Coronado explores Northern Texas.

- **1700s**   Spanish Franciscans establish missions throughout Texas.

- **1724**   Friar Antonio Olivares determines the final site for the Alamo.

- **1731**   Canary Islanders arrive in San Antonio to settle a new and permanent colony.

- **1738**   Catholic leaders lay the cornerstone for San Fernando Church.

- **1744**   Franciscans begin the first church at the Alamo.

- **1749**   Citizens complete construction of San Fernando Church.

- **1776**   English colonies sign the Declaration of Independence.

- **1813**   Juan Ximenes builds *La Capilla de los Milagros* in San Antonio.

- **1836**   Mexican army defeats the Texians at the fall of the Alamo.

- **1836**   Texas wins its independence at the Battle of San Jacinto and becomes a republic.

- **1844**   John McCullough and John Wesley DeVibiss hold the first Protestant religious service in San Antonio.

- **1845**   Texas joins the union as the twenty-eighth state.

- **1847**   John McCullough builds an adobe building, the First Presbyterian Church in San Antonio.

- **1849**   Episcopalians begin the organization of a new church.

- **1851**   Seven Ursuline Sisters arrive from New Orleans and Galveston to begin a Catholic school for young women.

- **1857**   Irish and German workers complete St. Mary's Catholic Church, the first English-speaking church in San Antonio.

- **1860**   Lutheran congregation establishes St. John's Church.

- **1861**   Civil War begins in the United States.

- **1861** The Confederate States of America accept Texas as a member.

- **1861** Rev. John H. Thurmond organizes The First Baptist Church of San Antonio.

- **1868** Catholic German immigrants lay the cornerstone for St. Joseph's Catholic Church.

- **1871** Parishioners complete St. Joseph's Catholic Church.

- **1878** Workers complete construction of The First Baptist Church of San Antonio.

- **1879** Methodists from Germany build the Little Church of La Villita.

- **1881** Episcopal congregation completes St. Mark's Episcopal Church.

- **1882** Rev. William Buchanan establishes Madison Square Presbyterian Church.

- **1883** Rev. David Pennington organizes Central Christian Church.

- **1883** Methodist congregation lays the cornerstone for Travis Park United Methodist Church.

- **1903** Construction begins on Grace English Evangelical Lutheran Church.

- **1910** Members begin erection of the present First Presbyterian Church.

- **1912** Claretian Congregation dedicates Immaculate Heart of Mary Catholic Church.

- **1921** The Great Flood takes the lives of many people and damages numerous churches in San Antonio.

- **1923** Parish members build the new St. Mary's Catholic Church.

- **1925** Baptist congregation builds the present First Baptist Church of San Antonio on McCullough Ave.

- **1927** Catholic Italian immigrants dedicate San Francesco di Paola Catholic Church.

- **1929** Worshipers complete new Grace English Evangelical Lutheran Church.

- **1931** Congregation constructs the most recent St. John's Lutheran Church.

PART ONE

**San Antonio Mission, Church, and Chapel
Constructed During the Period of
Spanish and Mexican Control
1719-1813**

MISSION SAN ANTONIO DE VALERO
THE ALAMO

LOCATION

The Alamo, formerly known as Mission San Antonio de Valero, is located on North Alamo Street between Houston Street and Commerce Street. It is next to the Menger Hotel and just east of the well known Alamo Plaza.

MISSION

Although the Alamo is no longer used for religious purposes, it is preserved as a national shrine. The Daughters of the Republic of Texas, under the direction of the Texas General Land Office, are dedicated to its preservation as a sacred memorial to the Alamo defenders. They are committed also to the conservation of the historic grounds and to the research of Texas history.

HISTORY

On an early Spanish expedition to the new world, Father Fray Damian Massanet, a Franciscan friar and missionary, offered a special Mass on a beautiful riverbank in central Tejas on June 13, 1691. The service was for the group of soldiers and priests that had been traveling with him throughout Tejas. Coincidentally, the celebration happened to fall on the feast day of St. Anthony de Padua. As a result, Father Massenet named the river, that was previously called the Yanaguana, the San Antonio River in honor of the Spanish saint. Future European explorers and missionaries often used the river as a resting and watering spot during their expeditions, leading ultimately to identifying the whole area as the City of San Antonio.

The creation of the present Alamo, originally known as Mission San Antonio de Valero, was primarily the work of the valiant Father Antonio Olivares, who for many years pushed for the establishment of a new mission along the San Antonio River. After two attempts to find a suitable location with access to irrigation, the final site on Alamo Plaza was selected in 1724.

During this mission period, the Franciscan missionaries attempted to teach the area's indigenous people their farming and ranching techniques. They introduced cattle, horses, pigs, and chickens. They also taught them how to read and write, how to weave, and how to work with metal using European tools. Of course, a primary goal was to teach them about the Catholic faith. They constructed a friary for the Franciscan priests and brothers, living quarters for the Native Americans, workshops where they could develop methods and tools for their trades, and stone fences for protection.

In 1744, a cornerstone was laid to mark the beginning of a stone church. The building, constructed in a traditional Tuscan style collapsed, however, and historians believe the destruction was the result of poor building methods and inadequate architectural designs. Work began on a new church in 1758, with a beautiful façade that featured many attractive carvings. Although the church was never fully completed and lacked a roof over the nave, it served for many years as a place of religious worship.

However, Spain always had a time limit for accomplishing the goals of the missions, and the regulations of the Spanish government along with continual problems caused by epidemics, attacks by some indigenous tribes, and lack of funding eventually led to the secularization of Mission San Antonio de Valero in 1793. All lands, tools, and seeds were divided among the local indigenous people. The formal efforts of the Franciscans to Christianize the Native Americans at the mission came to an end. The religious articles and records went to the parish church of San Fernando.

Under the control of the Spanish soldiers who now occupied the mission, the name was changed in the early 1800s to Alamo. The soldiers were largely from a Mexican town named *San Jose y Santiago del Alamo*. The word for the cottonwood tree in Spanish is *alamo*, and the trees surrounding the area reminded the soldiers of the trees of their home town. As a result, the mission was dubbed "Alamo," and the new identity stuck. In addition to serving as a military headquarters, the Alamo became the first hospital in Texas providing medical care for soldiers and local citizens.

After Mexican Independence in 1821, the Alamo continued to be used by various military groups and figured in several historic battles between the Texians and the Mexicans. In 1836, the Texians fought a successful battle against the troops led by Mexican General Martin Perfecto de Cos. The victorious volunteer Texians occupied the Alamo and decided to make the place their stand in the name of freedom from the oppressive Mexican government, a decision that proved to be disastrous, as all but one of the Texian soldiers were massacred in the bloody conflict that became known as The Battle of the Alamo.

Less than two months later, however, Texas won its independence by defeating the Mexican Army at the Battle of San Jacinto. After the surprising victory, Texas was quickly formed into a republic and remained under this governing system between 1836 and 1845. Control of the Alamo was transferred to Col. Juan Seguin of the newly formed army of the Texas Republic. Later, Col. Seguin gathered the remnants of the soldiers who died in the Alamo and respectfully buried them under the altar railing of San Fernando Church.

In 1845, Texas was admitted as the twenty-eighth state of the union, and from 1846 to 1861, the Alamo was occupied by U.S. military troops who placed a wooden roof on the structure. The famous bell-shaped parapet was designed to cover the V-shaped roof. The current concrete vaulted roof was designed and constructed in 1920. This addition is visible today in a mortar line that is just above the top niches, where statues had once been placed. The addition gives the distinctive look that is known all over the world.

When the Civil War erupted in 1861, Texas quickly joined the Confederacy with the support of Col. David E. Twiggs, and the Alamo became a hub of military activity under confederate control for four years. At the end of the war, the structure was returned to the control of the Catholic Church until 1883, when it was sold to the State of Texas for $20,000.

After that, a new battle began about the best way to preserve this hallowed place. In 1905, with the generous support of Clara Driscoll, the Daughters of the Republic of Texas were appointed custodians. They now manage the shrine as contractors for the Texas General Land office.

DESIGN–ARCHITECTURE

Alamo Plaza offers a clear view of the world-famous structure and is the spot where people come to be photographed for the celebration of weddings, anniversaries, birthdays, and vacations. It is also a favorite spot for political rallies. Although the Alamo is small and simple in design, it is the most frequently visited structure in Texas and one of the most visited in the United States.

The Alamo was constructed of large blocks of locally quarried limestone. On the façade are four niches that once held statues of St. Clare, St. Francis, St. Margaret of Cortona, and St. Dominic. The statues disappeared over the years and their whereabouts are unknown. A sculpture of Our Lady of the Immaculate Conception was never placed in the fifth niche as was planned by the Franciscan Friars. Intricate carvings can be seen above the doorway and niches. On the north side of the church, the window and door were sealed for better security.

Upon entering the Alamo, a sense of reverence is felt almost immediately. Perhaps the feeling exists because of the practice of the docents who ask men to remove their hats and for all to speak in hushed tones. The first small room to the right was originally a baptistery. It now holds a statue of St. Anthony, patron saint of San Antonio, and a bell that is said to be from the Missionary Era of 1719 to 1793. The room to the left was used as a confessional and now contains a stained glass work of art that depicts the Battle of the Alamo and a prayer stand donated by the family of an Alamo defender, Micajah Autry. The second room to the left served as a temporary sacristy and leads to the larger room that was used as a chapel because the main church was not finished. High on the south wall of this room are three protruding wooden stumps believed to have held a crucifix. The room contains artifacts of special interest, such as a rifle and a leather vest belonging to Davy Crockett as well as a biography of his life. On the floor is a log that is said to be from his log cabin home in Tennessee.

The church was built in a cruciform plan or in the shape of a cross. The nave is the long center part of the cross. Today, the nave has a tourist desk and the six flags that have flown over Texas, representing Spain, France, the United States, the Republic of Texas, Mexico, and the Confederate States.

The floor is made of flagstone but was originally made of packed earth. Toward the front of the church is the transept or the arms of the cruciform. The left one leads to the exit of the church, and the right one contains a model of the Alamo as it was during the 1836 battle. The altar area faces east to follow the rising sun and is adorned with bronze plaques that list the names of the defenders of the shrine. Cuts high up on the walls of the nave indicate where the second story was built by the U.S. Army. The very back of the altar area shows where a battery was positioned during the famous battle of 1836.

INTERESTING STORIES

On February 23, 1836, Mexican General Santa Anna took control of San Fernando Church and raised a red flag from its bell tower. The flag gave notice to the Texians of an oncoming battle in which no prisoners would be taken and that impending deaths of the victims were certain. On March 6, after holding on for thirteen days, and knowing it was certain that no more volunteers were coming, William Barrett Travis, the Texas commander, is said to have drawn a line in the ground with his sword. He purportedly asked the fewer than 200 soldiers if they were willing to stay and give their lives rather than surrender to Santa Anna. If they chose to stay, they were to step over the now famous line knowing that they faced a Mexican army of over 5,000. All but one accepted the challenge. Among the brave defenders were James Bowie and Davy Crockett. Their defeat was inevitable. The battle site became a great shrine to those who were willing to give their lives for the sake of freedom.

Another legend of the Alamo illustrates how frequently romance, love, and lust have played a role in human history. The Alamo was no exception to such intrigue. The construction of the mission church required the skills of a master mason, and a craftsman by the name of Antonio Tellos was chosen for the job. Tellos, however, was said to have been involved in a romance with a married woman by the name of Roza Guerra Tribino. Her husband was Matias Tribino. During their tumultuous marriage, they supposedly had a violent argument in which Roza threatened to have her husband killed. Later, her lover Antonio asked Matias to meet him by a corral of the mission. During the meeting, Tellos drew a gun and fatally shot Roza's husband. He then retreated to Mission San Antonio and hid within the church. Soldiers surrounded the place, but in the dark of night Tellos escaped. Although people recognized the reprehensible actions of Tellos, many believed that the loss of his direction as the head mason caused the quality of the construction work to decline and contributed to the collapse of the church in 1744.

SAN FERNANDO CATHEDRAL

LOCATION

The cathedral, originally known as San Fernando Church, is located at 115 Main Plaza between Commerce Street and West Market Street. The entry faces Main Plaza, while the back of the building is on Flores Street across from City Hall. The Bexar County Courthouse is just south of the cathedral.

MISSION

San Fernando Cathedral is an integral part of the spiritual and historic life of San Antonio. It is a gathering place for Catholics and members of the Christian community to hear the teachings of the Bible, to pray, and to celebrate the Eucharist as well as other sacraments of the Catholic religion. It is also a place of loving service to the needy and to the oppressed. Its long history makes it a continuing witness to San Antonio's spiritual heritage.

HISTORY

By the 16th and 17th centuries, a race was on between the English, the Spanish, the French, and the Portuguese to explore and claim the lands of the new world. To keep the French from claiming the remote territory of Tejas, the Spanish Council of the Indies recommended that several families from the Canary Islands be sent to help establish and to populate a permanent settlement in the vast Southwest. With the support of King Philip V, these families sailed to Cuba and then on to Veracruz, Mexico. From there they made an arduous journey over land to a small remote military outpost in the new world. On March 9, 1731, fifty-five weary Canary Islanders were presented to Juan Antonio de Almazan, Captain of the Presidio of San Antonio. Their arrival marked the beginning of La Villa de San Fernando. The Canary Island immigrants established a government of sorts and by the authority of the Spanish king, formal grants of land were awarded to the various families.

In 1738, a cornerstone was laid for the construction of San Fernando Church, establishing it as the first Catholic parish in Texas. Under the direction of the priests, the settlers and the soldiers were required to support and work on the construction of the church. It took more than ten years to complete the building that is now recognized as the oldest cathedral sanctuary in the United States. The original walls, some of the longest standing structures in Texas, are still intact. The doors of the original church mark the geographic point from which all surveying and mileage to San Antonio was and is still measured.

Several battles took place in the early history of San Antonio, and many of the army's casualties were interred in the church, which also contains the remains of San Antonio's first bishop, Anthony Dominic Pellicer. Most notably, some of the heroes of the Alamo were laid to rest there after the infamous battle in 1836. One hundred years later during a process of restoration, these remnants were discovered under the altar railing. They were removed and placed in a white marble sarcophagus that is now at the south entry of the cathedral. The bones and ashes are said to be those of Jim Bowie, who married Ursula de Veramendi at San Fernando in 1831; Davy Crockett; and William Barrett Travis. To this day, people from all over the world come to visit this historic tomb.

In 1868, an additional cornerstone was added to San Fernando marking a new addition to the church. The French Gothic Revival expansion was completed in 1873 and the following year Pope Pius IX declared San Fernando a cathedral. In 1978, in an effort to bring back the simple design of the original structure, another major restoration of the cathedral was undertaken by the famous architect O'Neil Ford.

However, San Fernando Cathedral is more than stone and mortar. It is the heart of San Antonio and has a Mexican flavor that includes the celebration of traditional feasts with mariachi music and Native American dance. In 1983, Father Virgilio Elizondo was the first San Antonio born rector. From his family background, Elizondo knew of the many religious traditions that existed among the Mexican people and made a determined effort to revive many of them among the parishioners, including the dramatization of The Passion which attracts 20,000 people each year to San Fernando Plaza. He developed also the internationally televised Sunday Mass which at its peak reached over seven million people.

In 1995, Father Elizondo was followed by Father David Garcia, who conducted a campaign that raised twenty-one million dollars for restoration of the cathedral as well as construction of the AT&T community center. He continued restoring old Spanish colonial customs and initiated a unique prayer service with a blessing of the mayor and City Council members. Together with Mayor Phil Hardberger, he expanded Main Plaza, that has become the heart of the city, and opened the Portal San Fernando on the Riverwalk with direct access to San Fernando Cathedral. Additional restorations have been made to the cathedral over the years, the latest taking place in 2001-2003, under Rafferty Rafferty Tollfeson with the associate architectural firm of Fisher Heck. At that time, the altar was moved to the center of the church to allow for better participation of the congregation.

On September 13, 1987, Pope John Paul II prayed and spoke in the cathedral. He is the only pope to visit the historic site. In 1966, President Lyndon Johnson paid a visit, as have governors, ambassadors, and countless foreign leaders. The installation in 2005 of Archbishop Jose Gomez, STD, was followed by the investiture in 2010 of Archbishop Gustavo Garcia-Siller, M.Sp.S. For nearly 300 years, the historic cathedral has continued to change and grow as a living spiritual treasure of San Antonio.

DESIGN–ARCHITECTURE

There are two distinct sections to San Fernando Cathedral. The original was built in Spanish Colonial style and the addition built in French Gothic Revival style. Main Plaza and Military Plaza offer excellent views of the two sections. From Military Plaza, the original Spanish Colonial style is the focus, while Main Plaza offers a clear view of the Gothic addition that has a slight resemblance to Notre Dame Cathedral in Paris.

The original church built by the early founders of San Antonio was completed in 1755. It was made of locally quarried limestone that was plastered and painted white. A dome, that is typical of Spanish Colonial architecture, was constructed on top of the building. The expansion of the structure was called for in anticipation of San Antonio being established as a diocese within the Catholic Church and the necessity for additional space to meet the needs of the growing congregation. The expansion began in

1868 and was completed in 1873. The addition was designed by Francois Giraud, a local French architect and surveyor who was also mayor of San Antonio.

The entry of the cathedral has three arched and coffered doors, above which is a statue of San Fernando, King of Spain, as well as a round rose window that is typical of those used in Gothic designs. Many quatrefoils and trefoils appear above the middle door and on the façade of the structure. Small buttresses are used to strengthen the heavy limestone walls. The year 1873 is cut into the top of the metal gutters to mark the completion of the construction. The church is adorned with two bell towers that are topped with crosses that provide a fitting finish to the symmetrical design.

The inside of the cathedral is a blend of simplicity and opulence. The plain limestone pillars, walls, and tiled floors offer a contrast to the high, faux painted ceilings and the many statues around the interior. The original colonial sanctuary contains a gleaming retablo gilded with twenty-four carat gold that measures twenty-four feet by eighteen feet. It contains a gold tabernacle as well as statues of Matthew, Mark, Luke, and John. On the right is a dressed statue of La Virgin de la Candelaria (Candlemas) and on the left a large image of Our Lady of Guadalupe, Patroness of the Americas.

The Stations of the Cross, installed in 1874, are painted cast metal. At the center entrance, there is an imposing statue of San Fernando as well as a black crucifix that is surrounded by hundreds of religious medals, photos, and candles. These mementos placed near the crucifix by visiting pilgrims symbolize thanksgiving for favors granted or petitions for special graces. Candles or veladoras, which are considered expressions of faith, line several places within the cathedral. Many statues are worn down by repeated touching and kissing on the part of the people who regularly come to pray.

On November 17, 2011, a new permanently affixed altar with relics of St. Anthony of Padua and Concepcion Cabrera de Armida (Concita), a Mexican mystic, was dedicated along with a new bishop's chair. Relocated to the front of the cathedral is a baptismal font donated by the King of Spain in 1759 and brought over land by wagon. It is still used for baptisms in the church. Other points of beauty in the cathedral are the stained glass windows and the large pipe organ built by George Kelgen of St. Louis, Missouri, that was installed in 1884. The organ itself looks like a small church made of dark wood. It is considered to be of great value because of its age, state of preservation, and tonal quality.

INTERESTING STORIES

In 1836, the highest point in San Antonio was the bell tower of the old San Fernando Church. Local legend has it that because of this distinction, a bell-ringer was assigned to ring the bells as a warning to the townspeople if he witnessed the approach of Mexican General Santa Anna and his troops.

The bell-ringer was said to be a nice fellow with a small character flaw – he liked to partake of alcohol. There was not a lot to do in the bell tower and drinking helped him pass the time. However, it also clouded his judgment. Stories are told of how he would spot some dust from a cowboy's horse or wagon and immediately ring the bell, causing people to panic and scatter! After several false bell-ringing episodes, San Antonians began to ignore the sound. According to local legend, on the day he rang the bell for the true arrival of Santa Anna, no one paid much attention, and San Fernando Church, along with the rest of the city, was quickly captured. Santa Anna's troops immediately seized the tower and raised the red flag of "no quarter" to let the Texians know that this battle would not take prisoners; it would be a fight to the death. The fate of the infamous bell-ringer remains unknown.

Another interesting moment in San Fernando Cathedral's great history happened in 1987 when Pope John Paul II visited San Antonio. This was an especially exciting event since it was the first time a Roman Catholic pope had ever been to the city. The cathedral was packed with many religious people awaiting his arrival. The building was filled with the aroma of two and a half million flowers that were donated by local florists. Felipa (Wimpie) Pena, a long time and faithful volunteer, was given the honor of opening the front cathedral doors for Pope John Paul II. Then he was greeted by the Rector, Father Virgilio Elizondo, with a big *abrazo* (hug). Father asked the

pope if he needed to freshen up. He responded "yes" and was taken to a special back room with a bed where he stayed for some time. No one gave a reason for the delay to the waiting guests, but it seemed that perhaps even a pope needed a little Texas siesta.

LA CAPILLA
DE LOS MILAGROS

LOCATION

This very small chapel is located on Haven for Hope Street off Interstate 35/10 on Exit 569 next to Garcia Park. It is near Haven for Hope, a large shelter for the homeless of the city. Parking is available next to Garcia Park.

MISSION

The chapel is a sacred place of prayer and worship of God. Although it is not used for religious ceremonies, it is open to the public and attracts many pilgrims of good faith who are searching for a place of religious devotion. Since the 1800s, it has remained under the private ownership of the Rodriquez family, descendants of Juan Ximenes, the original landholder and builder.

HISTORY

San Antonio, in the new millennium, is a bustling city filled with sprawling suburbs, endless traffic, and countless Mexican food restaurants. However, the area was once an unpopulated region where bison and deer roamed freely. It had ties to Spain and to the Native Americans of Texas. In 1718, Franciscan priests brought the Catholic faith to the region by introducing missions as places of worship and education. They were accompanied by Spanish soldiers and explorers, many of whom married the indigenous people and produced the mestizo or people of a mixture of Spanish and Native American backgrounds. They settled by rivers and started ranches and farms.

In 1719, Juan Ximenes, a mestizo, established his ranch on land, according to the Texas State Historic Association, where construction of the original Mission San Antonio de Valero (the Alamo) took place. Ximenes practiced the Catholic faith brought from Spain and regularly attended Mass at the mission. However, the chaos and the violence developing in the area presented great obstacles for him and subjected him and his family to very real dangers of being attacked, tortured, or even killed by marauding indigenous people. The story is told that Ximenes sought and was given permission to forgo his responsibility of attending weekly Mass at the mission. As an act of continued devotion, he built a small chapel in his ranch house that could be used by his family for daily prayer.

In the 1730s and 1740s, the Apaches and other tribes repeatedly attacked the Mission San Antonio de Valero. In the same era, an outbreak of smallpox and measles devastated the population of the mission. In the wake of these ongoing tragedies, the Native American population declined, and in 1793 support of the hierarchy of Spain was withdrawn.

When secularization of the Alamo occurred, several items in the mission, including a large crucifix, said to have been brought from Spain in 1716 by the Franciscan friars, were given to local people, particularly to Juan Ximenes for use in his family chapel. It is said that he was so moved by being given these precious objects that he personally carried the large crucifix on his back to his home, where it was cared for and treasured by his family.

In 1813, the religious items were placed in a chapel built by the Ximenes family. The small shrine gradually became a place of great devotion, and when several miracles were attributed to prayers offered within its walls, the structure became known as *La Capilla de los Milagros* (Chapel of Miracles). In 1927, the chapel burnt down but was rebuilt.

In the 1960s, leaders of the effort for urban renewal wanted to tear the chapel down. The Conservation Society and U.S. Representative Henry B. Gonzalez, however, halted its destruction. It is now listed on the National Registry of Historic Places.

DESIGN–ARCHITECTURE

This small colorful chapel is about the size of a single-car garage. It is constructed of burnt orange stucco with a pale green tin roof. A small steeple adorns the entry, and two small stained glass windows bring colorful light to the interior.

The inside of the chapel has a rounded ceiling similar to an army quonset hut building. The walls are made of plaster and are painted tan and cream. The chief point of interest is the compelling life-size crucifix of Jesus Christ that Ximenes is said to have received from Mission San Antonio de Valero. Referred to as *El Senor de los Milagros*, it is located prominently in the center of the altar with additional religious statues lining the walls surrounding it. Over the years, it has blackened with age and with exposure to the smoke from many candles used throughout the chapel. Several smaller altars are filled with more candles and statues of various sizes.

INTERESTING STORIES

Many stories of miracles are attributed to the crucifix, *El Senor.* One famous legend tells of a pilot who promised to come and pray once a year if he survived the dangers of World War II. He kept his promise, and it is said that his pilot's wings were placed within the chapel in thanksgiving for his survival throughout the war.

Another story involves a desperate mother who in the early 1920s was frantically praying to save her son who was condemned to die for a serious crime. She promised God that she would crawl on her knees from San Fernando Cathedral to *El Senor de los Mila-gros* as a show of faith, while praying that her son's life be spared. When people heard of her plans, they lined the streets and placed rugs in front of her as she crawled on her knees from San Fernando Cathedral to *El Senor de los Milagros* within the little chapel. Phenomenally, her son was pardoned at the very last minute.

Many more stories of faith, healing, and miracles have been attributed to *La Capilla de los Milagros* and *El Senor* crucifix. All of them illustrate the profound belief people have in the power of Jesus Christ.

PART TWO

Churches and Chapel Built During the
Era of the Republic of Texas
1847-1879

FIRST PRESBYTERIAN CHURCH

LOCATION

The First Presbyterian Church of San Antonio is situated at 404 North Alamo Street. It is just south of McCullough Avenue and north of Fourth Street.

MISSION

The official mission of First Presbyterian Church states that the congregation is dedicated to "renewing minds and redeeming lives with the steadfast love of Jesus Christ."

HISTORY

When a group of Canary Islanders came to settle in the area that would become San Antonio, the city was considered the main settlement in "Tejas." Population of the area fluctuated because of the many battles that took place between the Native Americans, the Spanish, the Mexicans, and the Texians. After Texas Independence, more significant and steady growth became possible.

During these early days, the remoteness, the wild gunmen, and the many saloons within the city were ongoing concerns of the settlers. In spite of the obstacles, many families chose to make this place their home and to create a decent life in this land of tough opportunities. As the city grew, the people yearned for places that would allow them to worship in their chosen religions. For Presbyterians, a few stalwart preachers, such as Rev. William Y. Allen, Rev. Hugh Wilson, and Rev. John McCullough, answered the call by becoming the earliest organizers of the Presbyterian church in Texas, particularly in San Antonio.

In 1844, Rev. John McCullough met and began traveling with Rev. John Wesley DeVilbiss, a young Methodist minister. Rev. McCullough later settled in San Antonio with his young wife, Lorena Sayer, and in 1847, built a small adobe church with his own hands. This was the first Protestant church in the city. McCullough generously shared it with people of various protestant faiths, when it was not in use by local Presbyterians.

Unfortunately, McCullough's ongoing health problems and the tragic death of his wife caused his departure from San Antonio, but his efforts were never forgotten. The seeds of his labor were planted, and other dedicated men and women took up the call to establish a church for San Antonio's growing community of Presbyterians, particularly those with political leanings to the South. When McCullough's original church fell into decline, a second church was built in 1879 under the leadership of Rev. R. F. Bunting. Its proximity to the infamous Buckhorn Saloon, however, caused ongoing problems forcing the church to find a new location.

In 1910, under the leadership of Dr. Arthur G. Jones, the congregation completed its present church. The new sanctuary cost $75,000 to construct plus $15,000 for the land, an impressive investment by the congregants. It was equally remarkable that the church was completely paid for by 1920. The zeal of the people who helped build the structure led to the later development of several other Presbyterian churches in the area and throughout Texas.

The First Presbyterian Church of San Antonio is extremely proud of its history and credits its continued growth to the many able pastors who have graciously guided the congregation. In recent years, Rev. Louis Zbinden (1971-2000) stands out not only as the longest-serving pastor but also as the leader who increased the number of sister churches in San Antonio while simultaneously developing a congregation of over 3,000 members.

Design—Architecture

The First Presbyterian religious complex encompasses the entire block on North Alamo Street between Fourth Street, McCullough Avenue, and Avenue B. The church sanctuary is on the corner of Alamo and Fourth Street, and one of the best ways to begin exploring the church is by viewing the main entrance from directly across the street. This view offers a sense of the High Gothic style of the whole building.

The structure was designed by Atlee B. Ayers, who was a well-known architect in the city at the time and whose work included San Antonio's Municipal Auditorium, Christ Episcopal Church, the Tower Life Building, and the Administrative Building, better known as the "Taj Majal," at Randolph Air Force Base.

Ayers chose to use rusticated limestone for the exterior of the church. The structure has two massive towers of different heights on each side of the three entry doors. The four-cornered towers are adorned with crosses on the top as well as several lancet windows. A spire was planned, but was never built, and the lack of the steeple contributes to the heaviness of the building. Broad stairs lead up to three large arched wooden doors. Above the center door on the façade of the building is a very large stained glass window, three lancet windows, and on top of the roofline is a Celtic cross.

On ground level, to the left of the entrance, a historical marker gives the background of the church. The cornerstone, placed in 1909, is located on Fourth Street. Several buttresses help support the exterior walls. The aspects of the stained glass windows and the religious representations of the stone shields convey the pride and the commitment of San Antonio's Presbyterians to their faith and to their church.

The entrance of the church leads to the narthex or a large foyer with doors that open to the Gothic style sanctuary. The narthex represents the outside world which leads to the sanctuary. There is a wide center aisle leading to the chancel that contains the exquisitely carved communion table of dark wood. This sacred table holds a Bible on a stand with two large candle holders on each side. Behind the communion table is a dramatic and large stained glass panel depicting the Ascension of Christ. The chancel area houses also a carved wooden pulpit and a baptismal font. The walls of the chancel are covered with dark wood paneling. A six-foot Celtic cross of bronze from the Isle of Iona off Scotland's western coast hangs suspended from the ceiling in front of the chancel. According to Rev. Zbinden, there may be only two other such crosses in the United States. On the border of the arched ceiling above the altar area are stone carvings of several shields and a crown symbolizing Christ the King.

The sides of the nave are covered with wooden paneling. The magnificent choir loft is made of wood also and contains a very large organ that was played by renowned San Antonio organist Dr. Bess Hieronymus, who was choirmaster for twenty-seven years at First Presbyterian Church. The organ has fifty-five ranks of pipes and was designed by Robert L. Sipe, Organ Builders of Dallas, who built the organ of the John F. Kennedy Center for the Performing Arts in Washington, D.C. The pews are a lighter color wood with carvings on the sides facing the center aisle, and the carpeting is grey and contains a pattern of light colored crosses. The chandeliers with red trim provide the lighting for the church. The remodeled sanctuary was consecrated May 5, 1968.

INTERESTING STORIES

In the last few decades, downtown San Antonio has increasingly become a haven for the area's homeless people. Many of them wander around the First Presbyterian Church located close to the Alamo. During Rev. Louis Zbinden's tenure as pastor of the church, he was often troubled by this situation. Quite regularly, as he made his way in and out of the church, he was approached for money by the indigent people gathered there, and he was puzzled about how to help them.

One very cold December morning in 1981, a homeless man was found frozen to death in the bushes of the church property. He was a man that Rev. Zbinden had seen earlier and who had approached him for money. This man's death had a profound effect on the pastor, who felt he must lead his church in responding to the growing problem of poverty and homelessness in the city. This commitment led to the founding of the San Antonio Metropolitan Ministries (SAMM) started in the basement of the First Presbyterian Church. Today the SAMM Ministries are a large service provider of care and shelter for the homeless in San Antonio. Later, Rev. Zbinden also helped form the Christian Assistance Ministry (CAM), an interfaith group that assists the homeless and low-income families with food, clothing, financial assistance, and counseling. The First Presbyterian Church of San Antonio was able to turn a tragic death into a ministry of service to people in need.

Another person who became important in developing a ministry of the First Presbyterian Church was San Antonio's "Radio Preacher," Dr. P. B. Hill. Dr. Hill was an energetic and vigorous pastor who came from Virginia to lead the First Presbyterian Church in 1922. He also became the chaplain of the famous Texas Rangers and loved wearing boots and a cowboy hat, as well as packing a gun.

Even during the Great Depression, Rev. Hill's efforts to preach never slowed down. In 1933, he became known around the state as the pioneer radio preacher when he delivered a sermon over WOAI, the first homily broadcast in Texas. He continued to deliver his radio program "The Church in the Hills" for more than twenty years, and his preaching reached people all over Texas and other parts of the United States. The radio ministry continues to this day. On June 1, 1955, when Rev. Hill was seventy-nine years of age, the Texas Legislature named him Poet Laureate of Texas. He was the first minister appointed to that post.

URSULINE ACADEMY AND CHAPEL

LOCATION

Ursuline Academy and Chapel (now the Southwest School of Art and Craft) are located at 300 Augusta Street bounded by St. Mary's Street, Convent Street, Augusta Street, and Navarro Street.

MISSION

The mission of the Ursuline Academy and Chapel stemmed from the undertaking of the founders, the Ursuline nuns who came from France to serve the educational needs of young Catholic women in Texas. The nuns were dedicated to offering even their own lives in living the Gospel of Jesus.

HISTORY

The academy, chapel, and convent are true treasures of San Antonio and have a long and interesting history. The founders had a reason, a dream, and a dedication to the education of young ladies. They came in response to a plea from Bishop John Marie

Odin, a French missionary who had arrived in Texas in 1840. Five years later the Republic of Texas became the twenty-eighth state of the Union. A growing number of Mexican, German, Irish, and French families were flooding into the region, bringing many children of all ages. It was imperative that education be provided for them.

Bishop Odin borrowed money to purchase twelve acres of land on the San Antonio River for construction of a convent and a school. He picked Francois Giraud, a local French architect, to design the building, and construction began in 1848. The scarcity of funds and materials caused Giraud to use a novel building method called *pise de terre*, a procedure that used river bottom clay that was compressed into brick-like blocks. The material was a great deal cheaper than stone yet strong enough to endure. Another local Frenchman, Jules Poinsard, became the builder.

A young French priest, Father Claude Marie Dubuis, enthu-

siastically volunteered as a missionary upon hearing the request of Bishop Odin and arrived in the new world on May 25, 1846, with eight other priests and three Ursuline nuns. Under his direction and after many delays and problems, the convent was ready for occupancy. On September 14, 1851, after an arduous trip, the intrepid French nuns escorted by Father Dubuis arrived from New Orleans and Galveston at the Urusline Convent and Academy in San Antonio. Their residence was definitely not what they envisioned, however. The unfinished building was filled with rubbish and chunks of mortar. It was surrounded by weeds and had plenty of scorpions but no furniture. Father Dubuis, who was a carpenter, painter, mason, and a tireless worker, toiled to make their convent livable. His pay was the glory of God and the corn pancakes that the nuns prepared for him. The enthusiastic and hard-working nuns also shared in the manual labor and had a school up and running in six weeks. They continued their work of educating young women in San Antonio for the next 114 years.

They developed a classic curriculum that included four languages, French, German, English, and Spanish, as well as religion, geography, history, botany, astronomy, philosophy, music, sewing, and drawing. During the Civil War, in spite of a cholera outbreak that claimed the lives of seventeen nuns, they continued their work in education. By the 1880s, they had eighty boarders and 250 day students, a new dormitory, and a beautiful chapel. They also established many meaningful student traditions, such as the *Servium* pin (I shall serve), a yearly spiritual retreat, and carefully supervised school dances. By 1951, the enrollment reached 500 students, and the Ursuline nuns celebrated 100 years of service in San Antonio.

During the 1960s, however, San Antonio experienced much growth in population particularly in new subdivisions outside the city limits. Despite the efforts of the Ursuline nuns, enrollment at the academy greatly declined. The city and times were indeed changing. The Ursuline nuns were preparing to change too. They bought property on Vance Jackson Road on the north side of the city, and in the autumn of 1961 opened the academy at its new location.

There was much discussion as to what would become of the old Ursuline Convent and Academy. Some developers proposed converting the structures into boutiques, offices, and a hotel. The Conservation Society, however, was most concerned about preserving the historic buildings and gardens. Emily Edwards, founder of the Conservation Society as well as an alumna of the academy, proposed a plan of using the buildings for an art center. After much negotiation, the academy was sold in 1965 to the San Antonio Conservation Society with plans for developing the Southwest School of Art and Craft.

DESIGN—ARCHITECTURE

An excellent viewing point of the chapel and school buildings is on the corner of Augusta Street and Giraud Street, by the parking lot of the San Antonio Public Library. The chapel was designed in French Gothic Revival style, constructed of limestone and topped with a stone cross. Leading into the chapel from this entrance is an often-photographed iron archway with Ursuline Academy in dark iron lettering. Iron grill work tops the stone walls and is similar to that used in the French Quarter of New Orleans.

It was through the main entrance gate that the general public entered to attend Mass in the cloistered world of the Ursuline nuns. Another entrance, called *Le Toure*, a small wooden turn-around, was located to the right of the public doors on Augusta Street. Because of their cloistered character, it was through this door that the nuns were linked to the outside world. Beggars frequently rang the bell at the door and the nuns placed bread for them in the turnaround. Donations to the academy were often left there in small containers. It is said, too, that infants abandoned by their parents were sometimes placed there to be cared for by the nuns.

The convent, school buildings, and chapel are located to the south of the main entrance. The structures are made of limestone, and one is topped with a weather vane and a large wooden steeple housing a clock with three sides. The oldest building that served as the convent and school is located at the arched stone entrance on the left. The original building was plastered, while the additions have been built of limestone. Both two-story academic buildings were constructed in Gothic Revival design with large porches and blue shuttered windows. Beautiful gardens and a fountain are located between these buildings. The chapel has a large iron bell on the metal roof and has modified buttresses to brace the weight of the limestone walls. A maroon door in the middle of the plastered building leads to a very large courtyard on the San Antonio River. This courtyard has beautiful landscaping, a grotto, and a gazebo. The setting is used frequently for weddings and other special events.

The chapel was built in 1867 and designed by Francois Giraud in French Gothic Revival style. Much of the original structure has been preserved and many of the stained glass windows are original and depict various saints as well as Father Claude Marie Dubuis. At one time, the floor was removed to provide room for air conditioning equipment, and it was discovered that an aqueduct built by the Franciscans ran under the building connecting it to the Alamo and to the other missions. This is the only remaining Spanish aqueduct in the United States.

The doors facing Augusta Street open to an area where the

public could be seated for religious services. The cloistered nuns sat behind a wooden lattice screen on the north side of the chapel. There was also a small chapel used for private prayer. Above this area was a balcony for the elderly and sick members of the community. The chapel is now used for weddings and many other events.

The first academic building and convent were used for classrooms, dormitories, and a student dining room. These rooms have been converted to art classrooms, catering areas, and a museum. The next dormitory built in 1866 was later converted to a convent in 1912. The quarters for the cloistered nuns were on the second floor and were connected to the chapel. Today, they serve as administration offices. On the first floor was the dining room and recreation area that is now used by the popular Copper Kitchen Restaurant, an art gallery, and a gift shop.

INTERESTING STORY

As stated above, the clock located on top of the convent has only three sides and there are three stories told of why a face was not placed on the north side of the steeple. The first reason offered is that the land to the north of the city was wilderness and it would probably never be developed. Only Native Americans lived to the north, and since they used the sun to tell time they had no need for a clock facing their lands. Ironically, the major development of San Antonio in recent years has been to the north.

Another reason offered for the three-sided clock was that severe storms came from the north, and it was feared that a clock facing in that direction would be damaged.

The third and perhaps the most preposterous explanation for the three-sided clock was that it was constructed during the period of unrest caused by the Civil War, and "No one wanted the Yankees to know the time of day."

TRAVIS PARK UNITED METHODIST CHURCH

LOCATION

Travis Park United Methodist Church is located on the corner of Navarro Street and Travis Street. It is across from the St Anthony Wyndham Hotel and just west of Travis Park.

MISSION

The mission of the church is stated in its official documents: "We believe the basic themes which run through the entire Biblical story and the core call for each of us to embody this in our own lives. Our mission at Travis Park is the practice of unconditional love and justice."

History

The colorful history of Travis Park United Methodist Church is intertwined with the establishment of Texas itself. The church's name evolved from that of William Barrett Travis, the legendary leader at the battle of the Alamo and one of the persons who helped bring the Methodist branch of Protestantism to Texas. Travis was born in South Carolina but was educated and married in Alabama. After a failed marriage, he decided to start over in Texas. He practiced law in Anahuac, a small town near Galveston. It was there that he became involved in fighting against Mexico's oppressive laws, particularly those that required Spanish as the official language and Catholicism as the required religion of the area. The settlers felt they had been cheated because of prior promises regarding these matters. This pursuit of specific rights and liberty started the cry of battle. As a lawyer, Travis became deeply involved in the crusade. He was commissioned a Colonel of the rebel Texas army and later became Commander of the troops at the famous battle of the Alamo. Here he gave his life at age twenty-seven to free Texas from the oppressive Mexican government.

This heroic action, however, was not all Travis did for Texas. In 1836, seven months before the fall of the Alamo, he pleaded in a persuasive letter to the New York Christian Advocate for the Methodist officials to send missionaries to the land he loved. Travis wrote, "I regret that the Methodist Church, which, with its excellent itinerant system has hitherto sent pioneers of the Gospel into almost every destitute portion of the globe, should have neglected so long this interesting country."

In 1842, six years after his death, his eloquent request was answered by the arrival of volunteer missionaries. The group included the bold and brave twenty-four-year-old John Wesley DeVilbiss, who was born in Maryland and educated in Ohio. DeVilbiss answered the urgent appeals of the Ohio Methodist

Conference to send missionaries to Texas. By way of the Mississippi River, he made it to Louisiana and went overland to Texas.

During his journey he met a Presbyterian preacher, John McCullough, who became his good friend and comrade. DeVilbiss and McCullough jointly held the first Protestant service in San Antonio with fifteen people attending. From that simple beginning, the quiet but energetic DeVilbiss took on many roles. He spoke English, Spanish, and German, a tremendous asset, as these were the major languages used in San Antonio at this time. He was a man of many talents, including carpentry, surveying, and handling a gun. At times, he was even a coroner and a saddler. He was a circuit rider preacher, with an area of over 400 square miles that he covered by horseback. He endured attacks by some Native Americans, desperados, and unreceptive settlers. He continued to persevere in his missionary efforts, however, and to preach the Methodist faith. He conducted worship services at the courthouse with seats and a pulpit that he built himself. In a wonderful ecumenical spirit, he worked with his friend John McCullough, preaching on alternate Sabbaths. It is said they often had to compete with the noise of local cockfighting.

In 1847, he bought a lot on the San Antonio River near La Villita, where he tried to build a church. His efforts were interrupted, however, by his transfer to

Rev. J. W. DeVilbiss

Rutersville in East Texas. Two years later, he returned to San Antonio, and in 1853 helped an early group of Methodists to erect the Paine Chapel on Soledad Street. He retired in 1871 from the Paine Chapel, but went on to build his last structure, Oak Island United Methodist Church, which still serves the people on the deep Southside of San Antonio on Loop 1604.

The Travis Park Methodist congregation worshipped at the Paine Church for thirty years, until growth called for a larger building. It was not an easy feat to raise money, but the leaders relentlessly asked for help and funds for a new church. Their hard work paid off, and a valuable piece of property on the corner of Navarro Street and Travis Street was purchased. On February 25, 1883, with hundreds of people in attendance, a most splendid occasion took place to celebrate the laying of the cornerstone for the new Travis Park United Methodist Church.

The work of the church expanded in 1894 with the building of the Methodist Mission Home in a downtown area of prostitution. One of the leaders of a house of ill repute was Madame Volvine, who at the time was grieving over the death of her daughter. When a member of the Methodist congregation invited her to attend Travis Park Church, she accepted. Here she experienced a conversion that led her to change her brothel into what eventually became the Methodist Mission Home, a safe home for prostitutes as well as other women and their children. With the help of the Methodist community, the Methodist Mission Home later became an adoption center and a source of services for women.

The congregation continued to grow in membership and service. Years later, however, with the declining population in the downtown neighborhoods and the birth of the suburbs, it faced new challenges. Nevertheless, Travis Park United Methodist Church continues to adapt to the needs of its congregation and to serve the people of San Antonio.

DESIGN—ARCHITECTURE

A very good view of this historic Methodist church is from the southwest corner of Travis Park. The structure was designed by a church member, Francis Crider, in Romanesque Revival architectural style. The walls of the church are made of large rectangular-shaped limestone blocks from nearby quarries north of San Antonio. The church faces east with entrances on Navarro and Travis Streets. It has a unique round tower with four shuttered windows topped with a very tall steeple and metal cross. Nine major stained glass windows have rounded arches; some are topped with round rose windows. Two crosses adorn the top of the roof.

The church is constructed close to the sidewalk and has pleasant surrounding gardens. The historical marker and the original cornerstone tell of the Paine Church and the architect, F. Crider. There are two main entries to this well known church. One is located on Navarro Street and the other on Travis Street. The latter entry leads to a large hallway with doors that open to the sanctuary with a large organ in the front of the chancel. The huge shiny metal pipes of the organ are trimmed with light aqua-painted wood. To the left of the organ is a large painting of the Ascension of Jesus. To the right is a beautiful stained glass image of the resurrected Christ with the words, "Peace be with you." A few steps lead up to a platform in the chancel which has a piano, a choir area, and an altar.

Two large stained glass windows are located to the left of the sanctuary. The window nearest the altar depicts Jesus as the Good Shepherd. The back window is in memory of Rev. J. W. Devilbiss and bears his image with information about his service to the Methodist church.

The building has very high ceilings with large lighting fixtures. It has a balcony with separate seats, while the lower level has wooden pews with mauve velvet cushions. The carpeting is of a matching mauve color. The high ceiling and the openness of the church provide a feeling of simple grandeur.

INTERESTING STORIES

In 1941, the Methodist congregation decided it needed more classrooms for Sunday school. The leaders looked for a practical and economical way to fulfill their needs and thought of digging out the area under the sanctuary. Following the example of stalwart Texas settlers, twenty men from the church dug for over three hours every night for two weeks. The Coca Cola Co. loaned them heavy boxes and a conveyer belt to move the dirt out of a street level window to a truck. With a cement floor, stabilizing posts, and other remodeling techniques, the classrooms became a reality.

Some years later, in 1955, Travis Park was afflicted by tragedy. A huge fire destroyed much of the sanctuary, the organ, and many pews. It also caused extensive smoke damage. The ecumenical spirit of John McCullough and John Wesley DeVilbiss was reborn. St. Mark's and First Presbyterian Church shared their facilities with Travis Park Church. The nearby Texas Theater, the St. Anthony Hotel, and the YMCA helped by providing meeting space for over three years. Travis Park United Methodist Church experienced the help, the love, and the courage of the early missionaries of Texas.

St. John's Evangelical Lutheran Church

LOCATION

St. John's Evangelical Lutheran Church is located on the corner of South Presa Street and East Nueva Street and is directly south of the shops of La Villita. It is west of Hemisfair Park.

MISSION

The dedication of the church is contained in the mission statement: "We are a community of Christian people who study the word of God and celebrate the sacraments to become what we are called to be. We want to provide support for one another and to be of service to those in need. We take pride in our rich heritage and move forward in our response to God's will." Today, St. John's Church stands as a symbol of the German Lutherans' resolve to work hard and to honor their firm beliefs. The church stands ready to welcome people to the love of Christ.

History

From 1836 to1846, Texas was the "Republic of Texas," and the newly independent area attracted a flood of immigrants from Germany, Poland, England, Ireland, and France, each group of people bringing with them a different language and a distinct culture. The German immigrants, in particular, had an especially significant impact on the development of San Antonio. The German migration occurred in waves, beginning in the 1830s. The initial settlers were largely peasant farmers who came to Texas in search of land and in an effort to escape the political and economic hardships of their country. They settled in a cluster of small towns known as the "German Belt" that stretched from Galveston to the Texas Hill Country.

In the 1840s, another wave of immigrants came in response to an initiative by German noblemen known as an *Adelsverein*, which was a plan to establish a German colony in the Republic of Texas, to rid Germany of some of its peasant farmers, and to settle them on a tract of land that the *Adelsverein* acquired in the Miller-Fisher land grant. The German noblemen believed they would be able to control the colony and enrich themselves from the resources generated there. The *Adelsverein* proved to have disastrous consequences, however, since the noblemen were ill prepared to care for the more than 6,000 Germans who arrived in Texas. They had not properly planned how to transport, to shelter, and to feed the immigrants. Also, they lacked a clear understanding of the resources it would take to cultivate the harsh territory they had acquired. Although they were able to establish two areas north of San Antonio, New Braunfels and Fredericksburg, nearly 3,000 of these 6,000 German immigrants died of starvation and disease as they made their way to Central Texas.

Since freedom of religion was one of the key reasons for the migration, the establishment of places of worship became a priority. While some of the people were Catholic or Jewish, most German colonizers were Lutherans. Knowing there were numerous Protestant settlers, several preachers came to establish new ministries. Other missionaries were assigned to the area by their denominations in Europe in response to reports describing the conditions in Texas.

Lutheran missionaries, such as Theobald Kleis and Phillip Friedrich Zizelmann, made their way to Central Texas. They had been assigned to do mission work by Pilgrims' Mission at St. Chrischona in Basel, Switzerland. Both men would go on to help establish scores of early Lutheran churches in Texas.

Pastor Zizelmann arrived in San Antonio by stagecoach in 1852. He had little money and knew no one in the community. Although there was initial indifference to his attempt to organize worship services, this audacious young man persisted in his efforts and held his first service for fifteen curious people. It is said that he was insulted at the lack of interest and even more alarmed that a few gunshots were heard during his efforts to evangelize the people of the region. Undaunted, he was determined to start a congregation of Lutheran believers.

Sometime later, he fell ill and had to leave his post in San Antonio. After spending some time recuperating in Castroville, he served in Fredericksburg, but he did not give up on San Antonio. When he returned, he began to ride a donkey to private homes to provide services to willing participants. Gradually, a following grew, and on January 16, 1856, a congregation of forty-four Lutheran worshipers was formed in San Antonio.

The congregation shared a belief in the importance of education, and they quickly resolved to start an elementary school, teaching classes in English and in German. Educating young people in their religion attracted them to worship services. Their membership gradually increased, and a cornerstone for a new church was laid on March 5, 1860. It was inscribed in German with the words *"Gott Allein die Ehre,"* meaning "To God Alone the Glory." Throughout the turbulent Civil War period from 1861 to 1865, construction of St. John's Lutheran Church slowed but never stopped, a tribute to the growing determination and resolve of this hardy group of people. Finally, the congregation erected a steeple on the church and topped it with a gleaming gilded weathervane.

During the first fifty years of its establishment, St John's continued to prosper. Under the leadership of many capable pastors, the church acquired land for a cemetery, constructed a school, and formed fraternal organizations. By the 1930s, growth and the widening of Nueva Street, however, created the need for a new church. Marvin Eickenroht, who helped design the San Pedro Playhouse and the buildings at the Witte Museum, was selected as the architect. Ground was broken, a new cornerstone laid, and in less than a year the new St. John's was finished. It was dedicated in 1931, which was also the year the church celebrated its seventy-fifth anniversary.

Over the next eighty years, St John's was a growing congregation of faithful worshipers. For the children of the congregation, baseball teams were started as well as a day school and the Cradle Roll program to support young families with children. Many other activities were established, including a choir, a coronation pageant, and a senior service program. St John's continues to serve as an integral part of San Antonio's downtown community by supporting many programs that help the needy, such as SAMM Ministries, an interfaith service for the homeless, and Christian Assistance Ministry (CAM), that assists homeless and low-income families. Such activities sustain the missionary vision of the church and its founding ministers who are remembered for their resourcefulness. The present leaders remain dedicated to sharing resources within and beyond their church.

DESIGN–ARCHITECTURE

Smooth stone and light brick were used for the building materials of the new St. John's Gothic Revival style church. Above the wooden double-door entrance are stone carvings rich with symbols, such as a cross for faith, an anchor for hope, and a heart for love. The façade of the church is graced with stained glass window panels depicting Moses and Isaiah of the Old Testament, as well as St. John and St. Peter, apostles of the New Testament. A stone cross tops the front wall and on the side is a seventy-foot bell tower. Many religious symbols adorn the outside walls of the tower including the alpha and omega, a dove, the hand of God, and the Star of David. Three bells which came from the original church and were cast in 1886 hang in the tower. The bells were symbolically named faith, hope, and love. The congregation has used these bells to announce the existence of Christ to the city of San Antonio for over 125 years.

The narthex of the structure has stained glass windows designed by Von Gerichten Studios of Colombus, Ohio, that illustrate the symbols of the sacraments. The nave is a classic Gothic design with clerestory above the arches that separate the side aisles. The backdrop or reredo, depicting the Last Supper, was carved by Alois Lang, a famous woodcarver who emigrated from Bavaria and is credited with bringing ecclesiastical woodcarving to the United States.

The large front stained glass panel contains many religious symbols, including representations of the Holy Trinity. Of special significance is a pelican depicted in the middle of the strained glass panel of the chancel. If unable to find food the bird is said to pluck open her own body and feed her brood with her blood, a symbol of Jesus saving mankind with His precious blood at the crucifixion. Other points of interest are the baptistery, the lectern, the pulpit, as well as twelve shields above the pillars of the sanctuary representing the twelve apostles. Just below the stained glass windows is a long stone molding decorated with five symbols: the rose (prophecy), the *fleur-de-lis* (incarnation), the pomegranate (resurrection), the shell (baptism), and grapes with wheat (communion). The symbols reflect the statement on the cornerstone of the church, "To God Alone the Glory."

INTERESTING STORY

The original weathervane atop the steeple of the first St. John's Lutheran Church was in the form of a gilded rooster. The large bird was commonly used to top churches in Europe as a reference to the story of Peter's denial of Jesus in the Agony of the Garden: "I say to you, Peter, the rooster will not crow today until you have denied three times that you know Me." (Luke 22:54-62) In San Antonio, a lack of cultural and Biblical understanding frequently made the rooster a source of ridicule, and St. John's was sometimes called the "Rooster Church." Some church members felt offended by the nickname, and in time, the rooster was replaced by a cross. Unfortunately, the gilded rooster has disappeared, but today, St. John's proudly embraces the symbol and often uses the name "Rooster Church" with great affection and pride.

ST. MARY'S CATHOLIC CHURCH

LOCATION

St. Mary's Catholic Church is located on the busy and narrow St. Mary's Street between Houston Street and Commerce Street. It is just north of the San Antonio Riverwalk and between two of San Antonio's landmarks, the Empire Theatre and the Aztec Theatre.

MISSION

The mission of St. Mary's Catholic Church is to provide for the basic spiritual needs of the downtown parish as well as those of the many tourists and visitors to the city. Special emphasis is placed on helping the homeless, the poor, and the hospitalized.

HISTORY

After 1718, most of San Antonio's Catholics attended worship services at the Alamo or at San Fernando Church. During that period, Mass was offered in Latin with a sermon in Spanish. By the early 1850s, the city's growing population included an increase in the number of non-Spanish-speaking citizens, and Catholic leaders began to hear complaints about using only Latin and Spanish in church services. Bishop John Odin and Father Claude Marie Dubuis attempted to address the problem by constructing a new church that would be available for people who preferred services in English. In 1856, after buying the land they needed from what was originally the Spanish Land Grant of Ambrosio Rodriguez, ground was broken and a cornerstone was laid for a new structure to be named St. Mary's Catholic Church.

Many of San Antonio's Irish and German settlers, who were persons highly skilled in carpentry and masonry, had a direct hand in the construction of the church of Gothic design. By 1857, work was completed and St. Mary's had its first Mass. The English-speaking congregation embraced the new church as its own place of worship.

In 1884, the Oblates of Mary Immaculate, a religious order of men, took over responsibility for the general upkeep and management of the structure. From this church they started *The Southern Messenger*, which was the first statewide Catholic newspaper in Texas. It was founded in 1891 by Father C.J. Smith, Pastor of St. Mary's, and originally called *St. Mary's Review*. Eventually, the newspaper became known as *The Alamo Messenger* and later became *Today's Catholic*.

This active parish began to expand, and plans were drawn up to build an elementary school in 1910 and a high school in 1913. Both were staffed by the Sisters of Divine Providence, whom Father Claude Marie Dubuis had recruited from France. St. Mary's

School was one of the first parochial schools in Texas in which students paid no tuition. The school was built on land that was formerly the home of John Twohig, a native of Ireland, a very wealthy businessman known for his kindness to the poor and to the Catholic Church. He generously donated his property to the Archdiocese of San Antonio.

After nearly sixty-four years of service, the original St. Mary's Church was damaged beyond repair in the historic San Antonio Flood of 1921. The flood covered the downtown area with over two feet of water, and more than fifty people lost their lives in the devastation.

As San Antonio recovered from the disaster, parishioners at St. Mary's were determined to rebuild the structure, and in 1923 laid the cornerstone for a new church. As a result of the lessons learned in the destructive flood, they took added measures to protect the building from future flooding by placing it on higher ground with fifteen steps leading up to the front doors of the church. The structure itself was designed by architect F. B. Gaenslen, who also designed St. Gerard's Church and the well-known Incarnate Word Motherhouse Chapel. The new St. Mary's Church was built with great strength and beauty and was finished in less than a year.

In addition to its beauty, the church embodies much of the interesting regional and international history that is part of San Antonio. Early Irish and German settlers, with the help of a dynamic French priest, had built the original St. Mary's Church. The new St. Mary's was designed with an Italian flair. It was built on the same land from an original Spanish land grant that was once a Mexican outpost. Today, the church stands proudly amid San Antonio's theaters, hotels, upscale restaurants, and the famous Riverwalk.

DESIGN—ARCHITECTURE
The church comes right up to the edge of the sidewalk of St. Mary's Street and College Street with the cornerstone located

where the two streets meet. The wording is in Latin, *Sanctae Mariae Ecclesia* (Church of St. Mary) and *Domus Dei et Porta Coeli* (House of God and Gate of Heaven). The edifice is difficult to view because of the narrow streets and high surrounding buildings; it is best seen from across the street. The building is constructed of tan brick and smooth stone blocks decorated with rounded arches. Above the center entrance on the upper part of the façade is a round stained glass window and a niche with a beautiful white statue of Mary. This detail is often missed because of the high location. A great deal of symmetry was used in designing the structure with two identical bell towers, one on each side of the building.

The design of the church is modified Romanesque and is modeled after the Sacred Heart Church in Lowell, Massachusetts. The interior has many arches and gilded ceilings decorated with different colors. The nave rises forty-six feet in height and is eighty-six feet in length. It can hold 1200 people, and for many years, it was the largest church in San Antonio.

The church emphasizes devotion to Mary, the mother of Jesus. A replica of the famous Pieta, found in St. Peter's Basilica in Rome, is on the left side of the sanctuary. Fifteen large stained glass windows depict the mysteries of the rosary. Large colorful reliefs on the walls depict the Stations of the Cross, while the smaller white tiles tell of the Seven Sorrows of Mary.

Statues of Mary, Our Lady of Guadalupe, St. Anthony, and St Joseph have been added to the structure. An impressive and not-to-be missed statue of St. Patrick stands in the front of the sanctuary and honors the influence and work of the Irish community in the building of the church. The main and side altars contain relics of the martyrs St. Athanasius, St. Theodore, St. Clementius, and St. Pius. The latest addition to St. Mary's Church is an exquisite shrine in honor of Our Lady of Lourdes that includes a majestic statue of Mary and a fountain of running water.

INTERESTING STORY

A special feature of the church building when it was constructed was a tunnel that ran under St. Mary's Street to connect St. Mary's School with the church. The tunnel was built to give the children a safe way to cross the street in the busy downtown area and to eliminate the congestion of traffic. In recent years, a hotel has replaced the school, and the tunnel has been closed.

There was always an air of mystery and rumors, however, surrounding the secret tunnel. One rumor was that it was really for the nuns and priests to meet clandestinely. As with many rumors, this story was never substantiated. Nevertheless, the tunnel was often a site for mischief on the part of some of the school pranksters who delighted in turning off the lights once all of the children were making their way to the outside. The tunnel became totally dark and pandemonium broke out. The sisters, in all their fury, could never find the guilty pupils who managed to shut off the lights, and no one ever confessed to the deed.

St. Mark's Episcopal Church

LOCATION

St. Mark's Episcopal Church is situated on Pecan Street between Navarro Street and Jefferson Street and is just north of Travis Park. It is across from the St. Anthony Wyndham Hotel.

MISSION

St. Mark's offers regular services of worship as well as programs in religious education and scripture studies to bring its members to a transforming relationship with Jesus Christ. Children and teenagers are an important part of parish life, and the church sees the God-given talents of the young parishioners as important resources needed by their families, their communities, and the world. St. Mark's Church is truly a place to pray, to find comfort, and to experience God's kingdom.

HISTORY

In the 1830s, San Antonio was a wild and rowdy place. It was the epitome of the Wild West with drinking, gambling, and prostitution. As the downtown area began to transition into a legitimate city, many new settlers recognized the need for law, order, religious leadership, and additional churches to civilize the growing population. Also, Texas Independence, in 1836, brought the dawn of freedom of religion for all and created the opportunity for Catholic and Protestant religions to flourish throughout the region.

For Episcopalians, formal attempts to establish a church in San Antonio began when Episcopal Missionary Bishop George Washington Freeman visited the town in 1848. Following the Mexican War, a number of military leaders with ties to the Episcopal faith settled in the frontier area. They longed for a place to formally practice their religion. After Bishop Freeman's visit, nearly a dozen families were admitted to the Texas Diocese of the Episcopal Church, and in 1850 they formed the congregation of Trinity Church. Two years later they had a full-time rector, the Rev. Charles Rottenstein. The challenge of starting a church, however, eventually took its toll on the small membership that was unable to complete its plans.

Yet the dream of creating a church of their own continued to be a priority with the families initially involved in the effort, and as San Antonio grew, more people became interested in the project. When Rev. Lucius D. Jones held Easter services for the group on April 4, 1858, the fledgling congregation felt renewed enthusiasm and once again began a campaign to build a church. Even today, the members of St. Mark's Episcopal Church of San Antonio consider this day as the day the congregation was established. The worshipers promptly petitioned the Episcopal Diocese of Texas and were formally recognized as St. Mark's Church. Rev.

Jones became the first rector of the church that now had forty members.

With the help of large donations from Samuel Maverick, James Vance, and David Vinton, land was purchased near a sandy square that later became Travis Park. These early Episcopalians were firmly committed to building a suitable and fine church that exemplified their strong faith. San Antonio, at the time, was largely considered an isolated frontier, and funds were scarce. The founders, however, wanted the best to create the plans for St. Mark's. They engaged Richard Upjohn, a nationally recognized architect and Episcopalian, who had designed Trinity Church in New York City. By 1859, he had a modest, yet very classical design for their church in Gothic Revival style. The building became Upjohn's only architectural work in Texas.

John H. Kampmann, the building contractor, used limestone quarried in an area of San Antonio that is now the Sunken Gardens and the San Antonio Zoo. A cornerstone was laid in 1859, and by that summer most of the walls were partially completed. The small congregation continued to raise funds for the church. Fellow Episcopalians stationed in San Antonio as U.S. Army officers provided invaluable support. Most notably, in 1860, General Robert E. Lee, who was then a lieutenant colonel in temporary command of the Department of Texas, attended services and supported the construction of the church. He was later forced to leave Texas and return to Virginia as the Civil War loomed, yet his support had great significance for the newly formed congregation. Even today, his participation remains a source of pride for many people associated with St. Mark's.

Unfortunately, construction of the church was halted as the Civil War began and resources became increasingly scarce. Supporters of St. Mark's, however, did not give up. They held worship services in rented rooms throughout San Antonio. Their steadfast commitment and faith ultimately made it possible to secure the funds needed to resume construction, and the first services at St. Mark's were held on Easter Sunday in 1875.

The church was consecrated in 1881 and became the cathedral church of the recently formed Missionary District of Western Texas under the leadership of Bishop Robert Elliott, who served there until his death in 1888. Bishop James Johnson followed, serving for only a brief period. His work was followed by the long tenure of Rev. Dean Walter Richardson, who stabilized the congregation. Although the designation as a cathedral would be short-lived, St. Mark's continued to expand in membership. The church was enlarged and a rectory and a parish hall were added. The Great Depression presented huge challenges, but the congregation survived with aggressive fundraising campaigns. During these efforts, St. Mark's frequently relied on the reverence and affection their supporters had for the past founders. Invoking the memory of Gen. Robert E. Lee was an effective way to rouse support. By 1955, the congregation had overcome many of its financial challenges, and the church had grown to be one of the largest and well recognized Episcopal parishes in the United States.

In the late 1960s, as San Antonio's neighborhoods began to change and families moved from the downtown areas into the growing suburbs, membership declined. However, today there remains a staunch loyalty to this great historic church that continues to serve and bring people together to learn the teachings of Jesus Christ.

DESIGN–ARCHITECTURE

Travis Park provides an excellent point for viewing this church. The architecture is based on early Anglican requirements that churches should be built from east to west with the altar on the east end, so that the congregation faces the rising sun. As was popular in the period, a return to the traditional Christian medieval form prompted the building of the church in the Gothic Revival design. The south and north walls, made of locally quarried limestone, have wide stained glass windows between the buttresses. Below the windows is a columbarium that holds the ashes of deceased church members.

On the east side of the church is a bell cote above a small wooden door that leads to the sacristy. The bell was cast from a bronze cannon buried near the Alamo on the property belonging to Samuel and Mary A. Maverick, who were founding members of the congregation. The bell holds great symbolic significance since it was once an instrument of violence and now is used to promote peace and love.

On the west side of the church is a large bell tower with an arched doorway leading to the narthex, and above it is a shield with a lion representing St. Mark. The tower and narthex were added in 1949 by noted San Antonio architect Henry Steinbower, who also designed St. Luke's Episcopal Church in Alamo Heights. All around the building are lovely gardens enclosed by iron and stone fencing. Near the entry of the edifice is a large pink granite memorial to General Robert E. Lee. There is a cloister leading from the main sanctuary to Bethlehem Chapel and to the parish hall that was designed by Alfred Giles in 1926. The historic St. Mark's Church and its grounds are a peaceful place in the midst of busy downtown San Antonio.

The narthex has several historic plaques including a noteworthy one that states the date of the marriage of Lyndon and Lady Bird Johnson in the church. The sanctuary has striking dark octagonal brown wooden columns with dramatic timber trusses containing many quatrefoil designs. Wood trusses support the roof over the seven-sided chancel. The apse contains lancet stained glass windows that portray the Holy Spirit and the four evangelists, Matthew, Mark, Luke, and John. Walnut doors on the sides of the altar area create a contrast with the white ceilings. A bishop's chair is located to the left of the altar, while on the right side is the pulpit elegantly carved by the former rector, Dean Walter Richardson.

St. Mark's was the site of the first organ in San Antonio. It was a hand-pumped model with rich tones and was purchased with contributions from army officers of Fort Sam Houston. The organ has since been replaced by a much larger modern instrument. Brass trumpets at the exit doors suggest an announcement of the word of God to all people. St. Mark's Episcopal Church was entered into the National Register of Historic Places in 1998.

INTERESTING STORIES

On November 17, 1934, San Antonio's well-known postmaster, Dan Quill, placed a special call to St. Mark's rector, Arthur McKinstry. Quill said he had a big favor to ask for a young man who was Secretary to Congressman Richard Kleberg of the King

Ranch family. The young man, Quill explained, wanted to get married on that very day. The rector told him that was quite impossible since holy matrimony was a serious matter and that a couple needed to have counseling prior to the ceremony. Dan Quill pleaded with him to reconsider and was finally successful in getting Rector McKinstry to perform the service.

The young couple arrived at the church at 6:00 p.m. As the ceremony began, the bride asked the groom, "You did buy a ring, didn't you?" The red-faced groom said, "Gee, I plumb forgot the ring." Supposedly, Dan Quill shouted that only Sears Department Store was open at this time. He rushed out the church door and quickly returned with ten wedding rings of assorted sizes, each valued at $1.50. The ceremony continued with little fanfare, no music or flowers, and only about ten persons present.

At the end of the wedding, Rector McKinstry whispered to Quill, "I doubt that this marriage will ever last." However, he was mistaken for on that day he married the future President Lyndon and Lady Bird Johnson. The marriage lasted thirty-nine years and played a significant part in the history of the nation. Their marriage ceremony is still recognized as one of the momentous events at St. Mark's Episcopal Church.

Another story that helps demonstrate the loyalty and affection many of the communicants at St. Mark's have for their church is that of Nellie Jane Lemon Shulman, a long-time member of the congregation. She was considered a true Southern belle who always conducted herself with dignity, modesty, and the manners of a lady. During the latter part of her life, she made it clear that she wanted her remains to be placed in the church's columbarium so she would never be late for church! Nellie Jane got her wish.

THE FIRST BAPTIST
CHURCH OF SAN ANTONIO

LOCATION

The First Baptist Church of San Antonio is located in the downtown area between Avenue A and Avenue B. It is south of McCullough Avenue and very near the Tobin Center for the Performing Arts (formerly the Municipal Auditorium).

MISSION

As stated in official documents, the mission of the church is "to follow Our Lord Jesus Christ and to lead all others to a joyful life with Him."

HISTORY

After the Battle of San Jacinto in 1836, in which Texas won its independence from Mexico, the search for the freedom of religious expression brought a flood of Christian preachers to the frontier. Among them was John H. Thurmond, a young minister who arrived in 1848. He was completely dedicated to spreading the gospel of Jesus Christ and rode hundreds of miles on horseback to expand his teaching through the wild lands of Texas. In 1861, he answered the call from the San Antonio Baptist Association to organize and establish The First Baptist Church of San Antonio. During the turbulent Civil War period, he was able to start a congregation of thirteen faithful members. The poor sanitary conditions and many difficulties took their toll on his health, however, and Thurmond died at age forty-three.

His work was continued by Rev. Joseph Creath, who made frequent trips by horseback to other parts of Texas to ask for money for the fledgling congregation's needs. He led the worshipers in beginning a church and a parsonage located on Jefferson Street and Travis Street. In 1878, with the combined efforts of Rev. Joseph Creath and Rev. William H. Dodson, The First Baptist Church was completed. It was located across from Travis Park, which was then surrounded by St. Mark's Episcopal Church, Travis Park United Methodist Church, and Temple Beth-El.

The congregation continued to prosper under the leadership of several capable pastors, and in 1905, to accommodate the growth of membership, a second church was completed. It was situated between Avenue A and Taylor Street, facing Fourth Street. In less than a year and a half the mortgage on the church was paid.

When World War I erupted and San Antonio became a hub for military training, The First Baptist Church reached out to the many soldiers. They offered entertainment in the evenings and invited the military to Sunday services.

There were several other Baptist churches in the city that were in need at the time, and The First Baptist Church helped each one by agreeing to pay one half of the debt incurred in construction or other expenditures. The legacy of mutual aid is a well-earned source of pride for the congregation.

On September 10, 1921, the great flood of San Antonio severely damaged the church and its furnishings. This disaster, along with growth in membership, led to another building expansion. In 1925, under the direction of Rev. Isaac Gates, a new structure was built. Rev. Gates also began an effective missionary endeavor by broadcasting services over radio station KTSA.

Some years later, Dr. Perry Webb answered the call to become pastor of The First Baptist Church of San Antonio. His moving sermons attracted record numbers of people to services. During his first year, there were often over 100 new members each week. By 1948, the congregation had over 8,000 members. In this same year President Harry S. Truman, member of a Baptist congregation in Missouri, visited and worshiped at the church.

Additional land was purchased for expansion, and over time an educational building, later named Webb Hall, as well as Kokernot Hall and West Hall were built. Dr. Webb served The First Baptist Church for twenty-five years and had one of the most fruitful pastorates in the history of the congregation.

In 1968, Dr. Jimmy Allen began his tenure at The First Baptist Church. He was a tireless worker, and under his leadership membership grew tremendously and several large projects were accomplished. The church started a valuable outreach program through live Sunday service broadcasts on KSAT-TV, a ministry enabled by the purchase of television equipment from The Today Show. The broadcast still reaches many people who cannot attend services. Dr. Allen established also the church's signature community ministries. The church collaborates with the San Antonio Baptist Association and Texas Baptist Men to perform service work for various disaster problems in the United States and other countries. In addition, the church has been involved with the Baptist

Memorial Hospital System, Baptist Children's Home, Baylor University, and many other institutions.

In 1996, Rev. T. Don Guthrie, the current pastor, began his service and has the second-longest tenure among the pastors of The First Baptist Church. He is a teaching preacher and models a lifestyle of both praying and service for his congregation.

DESIGN–ARCHITECTURE

The First Baptist Church's campus encompasses an entire city block between McCullough Avenue, Fourth Street, Avenue A, and Avenue B. The cornerstones from the first two churches have been preserved and placed on the walls of Wilson Chapel. The cornerstone of the present church, along with other cornerstones of the educational buildings and the chapels, are located on Fourth Street. The cornerstone for Kokernot Hall is on McCullough Avenue.

The present church was designed by local architect Will Noonan, who designed also the Maverick Building on Houston Street, which was later named the Buckhorn Museum. The sanctuary and lantern on the roof is octagonal in shape, made of massive masonry walls adorned with rounded arches characteristic of the Byzantine style of design. It is constructed of red brick with white and tan stone trim. The entry on Fourth Street has three rounded arched doors with white columns. Several arched windows are located near the roof line. On the east side of the entrance to the Great Hall is a porte-cochere in dark brown metal that allows easy access to the building. In the center of the campus is a large bell tower and steeple constructed of red brick to match the many other buildings.

There are several entrances to the church. The most frequently used are located on McCullough Avenue and on Avenue B. They both lead to the Great Hall that has pictures of all of the pastors who have served the church. The sanctuary is very large and open with seven stained glass squares in the ceiling, along with a very large octagonal-shaped one in the center. Stained glass windows in striking shades of blue and green have been placed on the side walls.

The front of the sanctuary has a pulpit, a grand piano, and an ample choir area that can accommodate up to 150 people. Behind the choir is the baptismal area. Facing the area on the floor level is an organ on the right with an orchestra section on the left. The sanctuary, including the balcony, seats over 1,500 people.

Unity Hall was constructed in 2002. It connects Webb Hall to Kokernot Hall and serves as an area for receptions, concerts, and meetings. The connection of the two buildings offers a unique view of the exterior walls. From the lofty ceiling hang large round iron chandeliers with matching rectangular iron light fixtures on the side walls that were designed by Kurt Voss, a long-time and faithful member of the congregation. The floors are made of over-sized stone tiles, and there is parlor-like seating on the south side of the hall.

INTERESTING STORIES

Interdenominational "Youth for Christ" meetings were quite popular in San Antonio in the mid 1940s, and in 1946 the youth leaders of The First Baptist Church were very involved in planning a special rally for the city to be held at the Municipal Auditorium. There was great excitement because of the music and of the dynamic young preacher who was coming to speak. Shortly before the event, however, an epidemic of polio broke out, and there was no vaccine to prevent the spread of the feared disease. The city ordered a complete quarantine of public gatherings and meetings, particularly those scheduled for children and teenagers. The planners of the Youth for Christ rally were devastated. In addition to the fact that the event offered great potential for inspiring many young people in their faith, tremendous costs for rentals, music, and a donation to the preacher would be lost. The young preacher, however, graciously refused any payment for his participation and offered to help in any way possible. Everyone deeply appreciated the kindness of this man. His name was William Franklin Graham, better known as Rev. Billy Graham.

The polio epidemic affected the lives of many people in the city. It had an impact also on the finances of The First Baptist Church. Children were quarantined from group activities, and families could not attend church services. Church contributions fell sharply. However, H. L. Kokernot, a cattleman and deacon, as well as a trustee of Baylor University, personally guaranteed sufficient money for the church to continue its ministry. In 1953, the church acknowledged his generosity by naming a new building Kokernot Hall.

ST. JOSEPH'S CATHOLIC CHURCH

LOCATION

St. Joseph's Catholic Church is located at 623 E. Commerce Street, one block south of the Alamo. The building is encircled by a large retail store formerly known as Joske's Department Store.

75

MISSION

The church serves a large multicultural parish of San Antonians as well as many tourists visiting the city. Since 1982, the priests of the Congregation of the Blessed Sacrament have directed the parish. In addition to the traditional celebration of Mass and the sacraments, Eucharistic Exposition and Adoration are held every weekday from 10:00 a.m. to 12:00 noon.

HISTORY

Established in 1868, St. Joseph's was the first Catholic Church in San Antonio to offer services in German and became a much-needed place to worship for San Antonio's booming German-speaking population. As described in the section on St. John's Evangelical Lutheran Church, a large immigration to Texas began in the early 1830s, as word spread that the state had an abundance of affordable farmland. The initial pioneers were peasant farmers who settled in a series of small farming towns and villages from Galveston to Central Texas.

In 1848, revolutions in Germany caused a second wave of immigrants to make their way to Texas. This group, known as the "48ers," came seeking political, economic, and religious freedom. Many of the settlers were either well-educated intellectuals or skilled laborers, and they came with more financial resources than previous immigrants. They were increasingly attracted to established towns like San Antonio or Galveston, where they could practice their professions or utilize their skills. Many of them were Catholic and seeking churches where they could comfortably continue the practice of their religion.

During this same period, Catholic leaders in Texas became concerned about the state of the Roman Catholic Church. The newly formed Republic of Texas had guaranteed religious freedom, but the revolutions and military conflicts, the isolation of some settlements, and the rough nature of frontier life had impacted many of the established Catholic churches. Religious leaders were aware of the need to bolster the faith of the Catholic people and at the same time to serve the needs of the immigrants.

In 1842, Father Jean Marie Odin, a Vincentian priest from France, was named Vicar Apostolic of Texas. He was assigned the work of rebuilding and strengthening the Catholic faith in Texas. He recruited the energetic and devoted Father Claude Marie Dubuis, also from France, and Father Leopold Moczygemba, a German-speaking Polish priest, to minister to the growing communities in San Antonio and the surrounding areas. He recruited also many religious orders such as the Oblates of Mary Immaculate, the Marianists, and the Ursulines.

At the time, most Catholics in San Antonio attended Mass at San Fernando Church, where the services were in Latin and the homilies were in Spanish. Many of the immigrants were familiar with the use of Latin in the church, but they did not speak Spanish. In an effort to minister to all Catholics regardless of their cultural differences, Father Dubuis had worked with German, Irish, and English settlers to help create St. Mary's Church. The church was built by the hands of the immigrant groups, and services were provided in Latin, in English, and occasionally in German.

By 1860, however, more than thirty percent of the population of San Antonio was German-speaking, and the people longed for sermons in their native tongue. Their growing numbers warranted a church of their own and they pressed on to create the type of church they had in Europe. They also possessed competent skills in masonry, carpentry, and bricklaying to make that vision a reality. With the support of Father Dubuis, who had now been appointed bishop, they laid a cornerstone in 1868 for a new church, appropriately named for St. Joseph, the saint who was a carpenter himself. In 1871, after much hard work, the church was ready for consecration and a large celebration that included a procession with a statue of St. Joseph and the ringing of the bells of San Fernando Church, St. Mary's Catholic Church, and the Polish Catholic Church of St. Michael, parishes that preceded St. Joseph's.

Improvements to the church by the industrious German settlers continued for years. Known for thrift and frugality, the community saved, worked, and waited for their desired additions. Finally in 1891, four bells with beautiful tones were installed and blessed. The following year, an all-male choir called the Liederkranz was started under the leadership of Father Henry Pfefferkorn.

The hard-working congregation later built a convent, two schools, and a parish hall complete with a bowling alley. The early church continues to serve the downtown area and has become a testament to the resolve and devotion of Texas' early German Catholic settlers.

DESIGN–ARCHITECTURE

The first architect for St. Joseph's Church was G. Freisleben. Later Theodore Giraud, brother of Francois Giraud, took over the project and completed the Gothic Revival design which reminded the Germans of the grand cathedrals of Europe. Under the direction of J. H. Kampmann, the edifice was constructed of limestone from local quarries. The cornerstone, dated 1868, was placed on the east side of the church near the front entrance with an inscription in German that translates "Behold the dwelling of God among men." On the other side is a dedication in Latin that translates "The house of God and entrance to heaven." A steeple made of wooden shingles and ornate copper work with a cross on top was completed by 1897. The copper has turned green with age and lends a distinctive finish to the church.

After years without proper windows, stained glass structures were purchased in 1902 from the Emil Frei Art Glass factory in Munich, Germany. The congregation paid $3,000 for these treasures that came to Galveston by boat and were brought safely over land by wagon. The windows behind the altar depict St. Ann, St. Joseph, and St. Boniface, who brought the Catholic faith to Germany.

Modified limestone buttresses support the heavy walls and are visible on both sides of the church. On the east side at the end of a stone pathway is a statue of St. Joseph with the Infant Jesus in his hands.

Inside the church, the Gothic style is carried out in the pointed arches and high ceilings. Behind the main altar are intricately carved high back panels or reredos that point upward and symbolize man's hope of eternal destiny. Surrounding the main altar are statues of St. Paul, St. Peter, the Blessed Virgin Mary, and St. John. On the left side of the high altar is a statue of the Immaculate Heart of Mary and on the right a statue of the Sacred Heart of Jesus.

On the left is the Altar of Reservation containing the Eucharist, which is similar to the Holy of Holies of the ancient Jewish temple of Jerusalem. The painting above the tabernacle shows the Ascension of Jesus into heaven. It is said to be the work of Father Henry Pefferkorn, a talented artist and the third pastor of the church.

To the far right of the main altar are statues of St. Anthony de Padua, St. Elizabeth, and St. Francis of Assisi. Above the statues is a painting of the Assumption of Mary into heaven, also said to have been painted by Father Pefferkorn. The church contains the Stations of the Cross with German titles.

INTERESTING STORY

In the 1940s, Joske's Department Store in downtown San Antonio started to grow rapidly and needed additional space. At the same time, families began to move away from the business areas and St. Joseph's schools, convent, and halls were no longer needed. Joske's took advantage of the situation and began aggressively buying property from the church. When they tried to purchase the church itself, however, the parish members, many of whom were descendants of the German founders, rose up and voted unanimously not to sell. St. Joseph's, therefore, became nestled into the middle of the department store that was constructed around it. That is the reason why many San Antonians jokingly called the church St. Joske's. Over the years, some people even thought that Joske's had its own church. Ironically, Joske's later went out of business, but St Joseph's Church remains open to proudly serve the people of San Antonio, and the Liederkranz still sings for services and religious concerts.

THE LITTLE CHURCH OF LA VILLITA

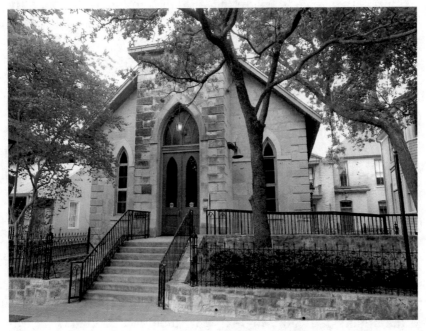

LOCATION

The Little Church of La Villita is located in downtown San Antonio between South Presa Street and South Alamo Street in the center of La Villita Arts Village. The church is on Villita Street near the Riverwalk, north of the Arneson Theatre.

MISSION

The church is not associated with any particular religious congregation but rather is dedicated to serving the spiritual, emotional, and physical needs of all persons who come to its doors. Without government funding of any kind, it is dependent on the generous contributions of the San Antonio community.

HISTORY

Like so many other churches and religious congregations developed in the 1800s, the Little Church of La Villita was established as part of the discovery of the new world by European powers that began to claim the vast lands in order to expand their empires. Spain sent Mexican soldiers to secure the borders of Tejas, and the Spanish government also provided royal land grants to Canary Islanders offering them permanent places for settlement.

Soldiers who intermarried with Native Americans, however, were not welcome to live on the lands that now belonged to the Islanders, who were identified with the Spanish royalty. They were, therefore, forced to move their families southeast, establishing an area that became known as *La Villita* (Little Village). They built *jacales* (primitive huts) and lived in this area until a large flood in 1819 destroyed the Village leaving many people homeless. In time, the villagers began to rebuild their homes, using brick and stone to safeguard them against another disaster. They were greatly encouraged by John Wesley DeVilbiss, a zealous young Methodist minister who volunteered to serve as a circuit-riding preacher in the untamed territory of Texas that included La Villita. He was a brave and courageous man with a tremendous love of God and a willingness to accept the challenges of burning heat, freezing cold, floods, and loneliness.

He had traveled with John McCullough, and their evangelical efforts led to the establishment of both the First Presbyterian Church and the Travis Park Methodist Church. Rev. DeVilbiss wanted to start a church also in La Villita and began by building a wooden rack to hold a bell that he rang to attract people to services. He became known to the Spanish-speaking people as *"el padre que tiene la campana,"* or "the father who has a bell." Unfortunately, DeVilbiss was forced to leave San Antonio for another assignment before he could construct his church. Not until 1879 was his dream fulfilled by a group of German Methodist immigrants who used their masonry skills to construct a very small church using local limestone. Many years later after the Civil War, the Episcopal Diocese of West Texas purchased the building and used it to establish the first Protestant church for African Americans in the area.

On week days, the structure was used as a school for the education and training of young women who were descendents of emancipated slaves. It was named the Bowden School in honor of Artemisia Bowden, daughter of a former slave, who worked at the school as a teacher and administrator for more than fifty-two years. The school began to grow, to become co-educational, and ultimately to become St. Philip's Junior College. It was one of the first colleges available to the African American community of San Antonio and the surrounding areas.

In the years that followed, several other ministries continued to use the little church until it was finally abandoned just after World War II. In 1956,  Rev. Paul Soupiset discovered the building which was now a locked-up and dilapidated structure owned by the city because of unpaid taxes. Soupiset settled the debt and began a special ministry to the poor, the homeless, and addicts of drugs and alcohol who lived in downtown San Antonio. His simple mission was to do all he could to lovingly feed and care for the downtrodden people, both physically and spiritually. He was relentless in his efforts to raise funds for his work, including taking a tin cup to businesses and street corners to ask for money. Locals dubbed him "The Beggar of La Villita." Undaunted, he went on to develop social welfare programs and services for those in need. Once he even went undercover as a hobo so that he could personally experience what life is like for the people he was trying to help. In 1963, he established San Antonio's "Starving Artist Art Show" in support of poor and unknown artists.

In 1965, after Rev. Soupiset's death, the Rev. David W. Edmunds became pastor of the church. He was an experienced leader who found ministry work very satisfying. In the early 1970s, a woman named Cleo Edwards Baros began to volunteer with Rev. Edmunds at the Little Church. The two kindred spirits fell in love and married. They continued their work at the church for nearly forty years. Even after Rev. Edmunds' death in 2002, his wife carried on the ministry of the non-denominational Little Church of La Villita. Today it continues to serve many citizens of San Antonio, especially the disadvantaged.

DESIGN–ARCHITECTURE

The Little Church of La Villita is small in size, measuring only forty-five feet in width and eighty feet in length. It was built in the Gothic Revival style. The limestone used for the church is believed to have been quarried from the area that is now the Sunken Gardens in Brackenridge Park. It is supposed that the large rocks were transported from the quarry on wagons pulled by burros. The church has casement windows that historians say were built by a Norwegian sailor named Olaf, who carved the pegs and hung the Gothic lancet windows himself.

An old, rusty bell hangs on the right side of the façade. The bell is no doubt reminiscent of the one used by DeVilbiss to alert people that services were about to start.

Inside the church is a stained glass window with a myriad of bright colors and a cross at its center. The window was installed in memory of Rev. Paul Soupiset. The church has simple floors constructed of wide roughly hewn boards. The little church can seat eighty people comfortably. The small size and simplicity of the chapel have an enduring charm that draws over 300 couples each year to choose it as the site for their weddings.

INTERESTING STORY

Rev. Paul Soupiset is said to have discovered his ministry of serving the poor one morning while watching television. As he listened to Dr. Norman Vincent Peale utter simple but powerful words, "Jesus Christ is the answer to your frustrations," Soupiset said he was brought to his knees and knew he needed to change things in his life.

He had been working in a woman's retail store in Houston but felt generally dissatisfied and unhappy. After hearing Dr. Peale's words, he felt called to minister to others, and decided to move to

San Antonio and start a new life. He joined a Methodist congregation and became so involved with his faith that he began to study to become a minister himself.

He discovered the unused La Villita church, which was run-down and neglected but just what he had been looking for. Later, he organized a place called Seniorville for older alcoholic men and a food program for people in need. Religious services held on Thursday and Sunday were open to everyone. Dr. Norman Vincent Peale's words changed the course of his life, brought him the happiness he was searching for, and enabled him to lift up the lives of many other people.

MADISON SQUARE PRESBYTERIAN CHURCH

LOCATION

The church is located on the corner of Camden Street and Lexington Street in the heart of San Antonio, just north of the Southwest School of Art and Craft.

MISSION

The church strives to be a witness to the unconditional love of Jesus Christ and to minister to the spiritual, emotional, intellectual, and physical needs of society. The congregation endeavors to seek justice and harmony in the world with the guidance of the Spirit of God. According to the published mission statement, it is "open and welcoming to all people, without regard to nationality, ethnicity, sexual orientation, or socio-economic status."

HISTORY

In 1881, Rev. William H. Buchanan came to San Antonio as a missionary for the Presbyterian Church of the United States. Although a church of that denomination had already been founded within the city, the congregation was somewhat divided between the supporters of the Confederacy and those of the Union.

Furthermore, the formal establishment of Fort Sam Houston as a permanent U.S. military installation gave rise to the idea that special religious services should be available to military families who had always supported the Union. It was primarily in response to these political divisions that Rev. Buchanan came to serve Presbyterians who had sympathized with the Union. Unfortunately, when he announced the first services would be held in a fire station, Major D. N. Bash from Fort Sam Houston was the only person who came. Buchanan was not discouraged, however, and soon had backers from the North and from within the military community. It was principally through the local support of prominent businessman George W. Brackenridge that he established the church. Even though originally from the North, Brackenridge made his fortune in cotton in South Texas during the 1850s and 1860s. He also established the First National Bank of San Antonio and became president of the San Antonio Water Works. Although some San Antonians never forgave him for his support of the Union, he remained a man of great influence within the city's business and military circles.

It was through Brackenridge's continued help that Buchanan acquired some land in San Antonio for the building of his church. The land was originally part of Joaquin Menchaca's Spanish land grant. On February 19, 1882, Buchanan and fourteen members organized a formal church. By-laws and a constitution were quickly adopted, and a board of trustees was appointed. Brackenridge served as a church trustee but never attended services.

His sister Eleanor was also a driving force in the fledging congregation. She organized and became President of the Ladies Aid Society, which passed a resolution calling for erection of a church building. George Konkle was the contractor and on November 30, 1882, the cornerstone was laid for Madison Square Presbyterian Church.

Rev. E. C. Scudder was the second pastor of the congregation and served during a disastrous storm that hit the city in 1886. Heavy rains destroyed much of the façade of the newly built church, as well as the tower, and interior furnishings. Through this difficult time, Central Christian Church shared its facilities with the congregation.

An appeal was made to the people of San Antonio for funds to rebuild the structure, and once again, George Brackenridge helped with donations of money and a tracker-type organ that used water for power. New members, John and Sarah French, were faithful and generous patrons who donated land for the parsonage and educational buildings. After her husband's death, Sarah also financed the building of a belfry with a 2600-lb. bell in memory of her husband. The church continued to grow in membership and particularly in extensive missionary work. In 1916, under the leadership of Pastor James M. Todd, the Assembly House for Sunday school meetings was dedicated. In 1938, Rev. Samuel Terry took over as pastor and remained in his position for over thirty-one years. This time of stability saw the membership grow rapidly, and by 1962, the congregation had over 900 members.

William P. Lytle became pastor in 1973 and served Madison Square Presbyterian Church for seventeen years. He was also elected the Moderator of the General Assembly, which is the highest position in the United Presbyterian Church in the United States. Equally notable, his wife Faith made an extraordinary contribution by organizing the first Habitat for Humanity affiliate in the United States.

In the last few years, the church has made an effort to include and ordain as deacons and elders people of different sexual orientations. Change in the downtown area and the development of the suburbs caused membership to decline, but Madison Square Presbyterian Church still reaches out to the people of San Antonio. The congregation celebrated its 130th anniversary on February 19, 2012, the exact day of its founding.

DESIGN–ARCHITECTURE

Madison Square Park across from the church affords a good view of the building. Limestone blocks, wood trim, and a pitched roof are used for the Gothic revival style of architecture. The church is symmetrically constructed according to a plan prescribed by the Presbyterian Board of Church Erection. A stone sign with the times of services, an historical marker, and a bell tower are on the corner of Lexington Street and Camden Street. The bell tower with lancet windows is surmounted with a steeple.

Steps lead to a pair of arched entry doors on the right and left of the façade of the building. Above the point of each door are lamps encased in iron designs. The sides of the edifice contain stained glass windows and modified buttresses to support the weight of the limestone. Large oak trees and shrubs surround the church and create a pleasant natural setting for the building.

A small narthex that contains a rope for the ringing of the church bell leads to the nave and chancel of the church. The nave is open and airy with high ceilings made of metal squares painted in pale green and cream colors. The chancel has a dark wood backdrop beneath the stained glass panels that depict Jesus Christ and contain symbols of the four evangelists, Matthew, Mark, Luke, and John. Other stained glass windows with religious symbols surround the sanctuary and provide ample lighting. The pulpit, lectern, and choir seats are made of dark wood. A stone baptismal font is in the center of the arched chancel. The walls are beige plaster in faux stone forms.

INTERESTING STORIES

One interesting tale associated with the early days of Madison Square Presbyterian Church involves Col. George W. Brackenridge, the shrewd businessman and philanthropist who was instrumental in the founding of the congregation. Col. Brackenridge had many and varied interests, including organ music, and in 1886, he donated a fine organ to the church and was duly recognized for his charity.

Unfortunately, he lost his own organ a short time later during the sale of his home, Fernridge, to the Sisters of Charity of the Incarnate Word. Brackenridge sold his home because he was grief-stricken over the death of his mother and no longer wanted to be surrounded by the memories of Fernridge. In the deed of sale, it was specified that he was offering the home and all of its contents to the prospective buyer. After signing the contract of

91

sale with the Incarnate Word sisters, he left San Antonio for a prolonged trip to Europe. Upon his return, he came to Fernridge in his buggy to retrieve his leather-bound books and his organ. He was informed by the sisters, however, that the items were legally theirs according to the terms of the sale. Brackenridge was very annoyed and offered to buy them back but dropped the idea when the sisters set the price at $3000. According to Sibley's biography, the Colonel declared at his bank, "Those old maids stole my library." It was said that he believed he would eventually get his home and furnishings back as he did not think the sisters would make all the payments of the contract. However, he underestimated the tenacity of the sisters who never missed nor were ever late in settling the terms of the sale.

Another interesting story associated with the church is that of Forrest Fitzhugh, whose grandparents and parents were faithful members of the congregation. He often attended services sitting on the lap of his grandmother, and Sunday school was a special time for him. His faithful attendance was rewarded with an eleven-year perfect-attendance pin. He also loved helping John Boone, the custodian, ring the church bell. With a boost from the caretaker, he grabbed a high knot in the thick rope, and as the bell rang, it carried the youngster up and down on a fun ten-foot ride, his feet dangling in the air, much to the amusement of the people arriving for services. Forrest went on in his relationship with the church through baptism, confirmation, marriage, and ultimately ordination to the ministry.

CENTRAL CHRISTIAN CHURCH

LOCATION

Central Christian Church is located at 720 North Main Avenue at the intersection of Main Avenue and Camden Street. It is just north of Romana Plaza, the Baptist Hospital, and the San Antonio Central Library.

MISSION

The mission of this church is the proclamation of the Gospel of Jesus Christ in all areas of life and work, witnessing in all situations to the grace of God in Jesus Christ. Members seek in all persons a response in faith and commitment to Jesus.

HISTORY

In the early days of San Antonio, settlers were lured to the area because of its vast lands, economic prospects, and the opportunities for religious and political freedom. At the same time, the city was emerging as a military stronghold, and the increasing number of troops added to the growing population. In 1881, the arrival of the International Great Northern Railway, a part of the Missouri Pacific rail system, established a railroad association with the city that transformed the slow-paced town into a burgeoning center of commerce. The connection helped strengthen the livestock and mohair industries. It also allowed the city to establish flour and grist mills; foundries and machine shops; tanneries; and brick, tile, and cement plants. In 1883, the first brewery was established, capitalizing on the bountiful spring water available in the area. The population swelled to 30,000 people. Gas and electricity lines were introduced and nearly 300 telephones were connected. The progress and modernization of San Antonio made it the second largest city in Texas and an enticing place to live.

As has long been true of San Antonio, however, religious leaders were often drawn to the city for different reasons. It had a lingering reputation for being open to gambling, saloons, and vaudeville. It had a red-light district that had long troubled religious leaders. For many preachers, new settlers to San Antonio meant there were more souls to lead to Jesus Christ. It was in that tradition that the evangelist David Pennington arrived in the city in 1883, representing the Disciples of Christ.

Pennington was born in Carthage, Missouri, and was described as tall, bearded, and in his mid-forties. He began preaching on street corners, in parks, and at private residences. After six months of devoted work, he had about forty-five followers, mostly poor women. He had hoped to establish a church and the necessity of doing so became more urgent when the San Antonio City Council passed an ordinance prohibiting preaching in parks. For Pennington, building a church seemed like a daunting task. He was having a difficult time making a living and his followers were for the most part very poor. He seriously considered giving up his ministry until on March 3, 1884, he was informed that land had been generously donated by Miss Martha Richardson for the purpose of building a church in the area. Use of this lot as security enabled the small congregation to purchase a more desirable location on Main Street and Camden Street, and Pennington oversaw the construction of a small frame sanctuary. On July 6, 1884, after much hard work and perseverance, the first Central Christian Church was dedicated.

Two years later a terrible storm raged through San Antonio. The small Central Christian Church fortunately was not damaged, but the neighboring Madison Square Presbyterian Church was devastated. Understanding the importance of having a place to worship, the members of Central Christian Church invited the Madison Square Presbyterian congregation to use their sanctuary until the church could be restored. This act of ecumenical kindness was not forgotten.

During the first ten years of the Central Christian Church's existence, over twenty-nine ministers served the congregation. In the 1900s, however, church leaders served with increasing longevity. Rev. Homer T. Wilson was the minister from 1901 to 1905 and under his leadership a new church was built. He was followed by Rev. Hugh McLellan, whose appointment lasted ten years. He encouraged the congregation to support members of the military based in San Antonio as well as refugees from Mexico.

As membership grew, the worshipers determined that a larger structure was needed. Although the shortage of building materials during World War II delayed construction, the membership's commitment to building a bigger edifice remained steadfast. In keeping with the vision, on January 29, 1950, the present Central Christian Church was dedicated under the leadership of Dr. Floyd Allen Bush. After ten years as pastor and forty-four years of service with the Disciples of Christ, he retired on October 2, 1950. Rev. W. Earl Waldrop followed and was minister for fourteen years. By this time, the membership had grown to 2,500, and the church enjoyed financial stability. Rev. Thomas S. Youngblood followed and was installed as minister of Central Christian Church in 1971. His unique style of preaching often involved direct discussion with church members during the service that brought a spiritual resurgence to the congregation. Although the growth of San Antonio's suburbs has caused a decline in membership in recent years, there is still a strong loyalty to this historic church.

DESIGN–ARCHITECTURE

The Central Christian Church is designed in a Neoclassical style. The façade of the structure has tall columns with symbols representing Matthew, Mark, Luke, and John. Above the Doric columns is a triangular pediment with a Bible in the center. Continuing upward is a very tall belfry with a copper-covered spire topped by a Celtic cross that is visible from many downtown streets. Several large and treasured stained glass windows adorn the building which is made of cream-colored brick and stone. Broad steps with iron railings lead to the large doors that are typical of this style. An historical marker and cornerstone are on the right side of the church in an area named Tranquility Garden.

Henry Steinbomer, who also designed St Luke's Episcopal Church and School in Alamo Heights near Olmos Dam, was the architect. Christy and Baskett, Inc. were the general contractors.

An ample narthex, which is made of walnut and large glass panels leads to the nave and chancel. The sanctuary is wide and lofty with cream-colored walls and a ceiling with elaborate patterns of dark walnut beams. The sides of the altar area have panels of walnut wood that match the intricately carved communion table. Jesus Christ is depicted in a large stained glass panel in the center back wall of the chancel. Beneath this section is another stained-glass panel that can be moved to reveal a place for baptisms. The large and rounded windows depict scenes from the Bible, such as Moses with the Ten Commandments, Jesus as the Good Shepherd,

97

and the Agony in the Garden. The church, including the balcony, seats 700 persons.

INTERESTING STORIES

In 1948, the congregation of Central Christian Church was making plans for the construction of the new building. They worried about where the flock could worship during the expansion period. The leaders of Temple Beth-El heard of their need, and Rabbi David Jacobson offered them free use of the temple to hold their regular Sunday services. Rabbi Jacobson, temple leaders, and many members of the synagogue attended the opening services. What was to be a one-year phase turned out to be nearly a two-year period. In addition, the Bexar County Medical Society and the American Legion Home offered the church rooms for their Sunday school classes. Madison Square Presbyterian Church shared space for their scout meetings and First Presbyterian Church allocated office space. In its earliest days, Central Christian Church had demonstrated the power of an ecumenical spirit by sharing its sanctuary with Madison Square Presbyterian Church. During this time of transition, that same ecumenical spirit enveloped their own congregation when they needed it most.

Throughout its 129-year history, Central Christian Church has received many donations including an instrument known as a carillon that was the gift of Mr. and Mrs. Lester A. Nordan. It is the only instrument of its kind in San Antonio. Carillons are often noted for being the largest known musical instrument, weighing up to 100 tons. This unique mechanism is composed of 23 or more bells of various sizes that are connected with wires and levers to the metal clappers of the bell. It is played by hitting keys or batons with fists. The connected wires make the clappers strike the bell thus creating sounds that form a melody. The batons are organized in the form of a keyboard. The carillon at Central Christian Church has 48 bells and is considered quite large in the world of carillons. The weight of the individual bells ranges from nineteen to 3,900 pounds. Since 1958, George Gregory, a member of the congregation, has served as carillonneur providing beautiful music for services and concerts.

PART THREE

Churches Constructed at the
Turn of the Century
1903-1927

GRACE ENGLISH
EVANGELICAL
LUTHERAN CHURCH

LOCATION

Grace Lutheran Church, as it is popularly known, is located on the corner of McCullough Avenue and Avenue E. It is just east of the First Presbyterian Church.

MISSION

As stated in the official records, "The vision of Grace Lutheran Church is that we grow as a light shining throughout the community reflecting the love of Jesus Christ."

HISTORY

The new influx of German pioneers and settlers in Texas in the 1800s had a profound influence on the founding of Grace Lutheran Church, just as it had led to the beginning of both St.

John's Evangelical Lutheran church and St. Joseph's Catholic Church. They had become aware of the opportunities in Texas through the publication of several letters by Johann Friedrich Ernst, who in 1832 had moved to the Stephen F. Austin Colony. He sent compelling letters to his friends extolling the virtues of Texas with its beautiful landscape, abundance of wild game, and affordable availability of land. His passion for Texas and his willingness to aid the new settlers earned him the title, "The Father of the Texas German Immigrants." Over a million people fled their native land and moved to the United States. A significant number chose to settle in San Antonio and the surrounding areas.

As Lutheran leaders of the Pilgrim's Mission Institute of St. Chrischonas near Basle, Switzerland, became aware that many of the settlers in Texas had no place to worship, they began to send missionaries to start churches. Their work led to the establishment in 1851 of the First Evangelical Lutheran Synod of Texas.

The influx of German immigrants increased after the Civil War. They were as diverse as Germany itself and tended to cluster in groups that allowed them to continue their religious, cultural, and ideological traditions. By 1900, however, cultural and language integration began to change within many of the traditionally tight-knit German communities. Across the United States, there was a growing movement calling for immigrant groups to identify themselves as Americans instead of the ethnic group of their origins.

President Theodore Roosevelt, in 1919, issued a call for integration in a letter he wrote to the President of the American Defense Society. It was read publicly at a meeting on January 5 of that year, just one day before he died. His urgent message was: "We have room for but one language in this country and that is the English language, for we intend to see that the crucible turns our people out as Americans, of American nationality, and not as dwellers in a polyglot boarding house."

Some ethnic groups, however, were not anxious for change. St. John's Lutheran Church conducted services exclusively in German, and although younger generations were adopting English, most of the founding members of the church wanted to maintain the use of German. The division led ultimately in 1903 to a group of twenty-three charter members establishing the Grace English Evangelical Lutheran Church under the leadership of Pastor C. B. Gohdes.

To begin their new church the group bought land for $1500 on the corner of Avenue E and McCullough Avenue. Soon after, they found a small vacant church building which they purchased for the bargain price of $1000. The building was carefully taken apart and reassembled on the new tract of land. It was used for worship services in English for over twenty-five years.

The congregation organized a choir and started mission groups to help form other Lutheran churches throughout Texas. In 1913, they began ministering to the sick by establishing the Grace Lutheran Sanatorium for victims of tuberculosis. The facility later became Lutheran General Hospital.

With a growing membership and a strong commitment to its ministries, the congregation decided to build a larger sanctuary. To design the new Grace Lutheran Church, they commissioned a prominent architect, Ralph H. Cameron, who had designed the Medical Arts Building, later known as the Emily Morgan Hotel. Jack P. Haynes, an outstanding contractor, began construction on the building, and the modified Gothic style church was formally dedicated on April 7, 1929, with a procession led by Dr. Paul F. Hein and other clergymen.

In the early days, the church faced many challenges, such as the Great Depression of the 1930s and a fire that broke out in 1977. However, it continued to grow and at one time had a membership of 1,400. Like many churches in the downtown area, however, Grace Lutheran was affected by the significant development of suburban neighborhoods. As the area around the church changed, and poverty and homelessness impacted the inner city, Grace Lutheran responded by becoming involved in the Christian Assistance Ministry (CAM), which provided food, clothing, and counseling to the needy. With a dedicated core of supporters, under the leadership of Rev. Christopher Gentile, other ministries were started to help the poor, the elderly, Alzheimer's patients, and needy children.

DESIGN–ARCHITECTURE

The present Grace Lutheran Church is constructed of a combination of tan brick and cream blocks made of stone. The fifteen steps that lead to the entrance are made of Indiana limestone. There is a large, impressive bell tower that features the cornerstone of the church on the west side. It reads, "Other foundation can no man lay than that is laid, which is Jesus Christ." A smaller tower to the east contains stairs to the balcony and is topped with copper steeple and a cross. Above the entrance doors are carvings of angels, grapevines, and shields. Also, there is a carving of Martin Luther on the roof line of the west side of the Church, along with stone angel-head carvings on both sides of the church. Facing the parking lot is a restful garden area enclosed by a black wrought iron fence.

The interior of the church was carefully designed to highlight many magnificent and symbolic features. The main attraction is the altar and an exquisite carving of the Last Supper, modeled after the famous painting by Leonardo Da Vinci. Communion is celebrated on the altar that stands in front of the delicately carved wooden reredos in the very rear of the chancel. On each side of the altar are two wooden angels holding candles.

Waldine A. Tauch designed and molded the baptismal font

in New York City in the studio of the famous sculptor, Pompeo Coppini. In 1925, the basin and kneeling angel were cast in bronze with the base reading, "One Lord, One Faith, One Baptism."

The ceiling has massive white oak beams stained a rich brown color that are supported by carved angel heads. The front of the balcony and the trim around the windows is made of wood of the same material as the beams. The chandeliers made of wrought iron and bronze fit perfectly with the Gothic design.

The tracery of the stained glass windows is of fourteenth century design. The windows depict scenes from the life of Jesus Christ. Because of its beauty, the building is often called the jewel box church of San Antonio and is a popular place for weddings.

INTERESTING STORIES

One definition of "grace" is goodwill, favor, or thoughtfulness toward others. Although Grace Lutheran Church has been a source of grace for many people during its 107 years of existence, the leaders are quick to point out that the church itself has been fortunate in receiving many graces over the years.

One outstanding favor was granted at the time of the cornerstone-laying service in February, 1928. Two weeks before, the church's Building and Finance Committee had met and decided that the educational wing of the church was to be omitted from the plans because of a lack of an additional $9,000 needed to complete the work. As word spread on the day of the laying of the cornerstone, one member of the congregation quietly approached Pastor Paul Hein and stated that he would pay the full amount of the money needed for the new wing. The member specified that his name was never to be mentioned, and to the present day the donor remains unknown to all, except to Pastor Hein.

The church received another extraordinary favor in 1993 as it was undergoing financial difficulties that threatened the continuation of several of its charitable outreach programs. The church was notified that it was mentioned in the will of a past strong supporting member, Vernie Walker. After her husband's death, Mrs. Walker moved to Fort Worth to be with her family, and although she had little contact with Grace Lutheran Church, it evidently remained in her heart. After her death, the church received a gift of more than $1,000,000 and the Grace Endowment Fund was created, enabling the church to continue many of its charitable programs.

IMMACULATE HEART OF MARY CHURCH

LOCATION

Immaculate Heart of Mary Catholic Church is located on Santa Rosa Street south of Cesar Chavez Street. The structure faces Urban Loop and Expressway 10/35, just four blocks southwest of San Fernando Cathedral.

Mission

The Catholic church is a home for all and maintains a multicultural heritage. It is dedicated to bringing people to God through scripture and the celebration of the sacraments, while addressing the spiritual needs of the poor, the young, the elderly, the physically challenged, and the family.

History

The start of the twentieth century ushered in a new political age for San Antonio with many changes created by its proximity to Mexico, where a long history of invasion, war, and oppression had resulted in poverty, illiteracy, and other social problems. There was a caste system in Mexico that consisted of creoles, mestizos, and Native Americans. The creoles were of mostly pure European blood and were about fifteen percent of the population, but they controlled most of the land and political power. The mestizos were a mix of European and indigenous people and represented about fifty percent of the people of Mexico. Lastly, the Native American people comprised about thirty-five percent of the country. The mestizos and particularly the indigenous people found it very difficult to improve their lives because of the political and social system.

In the early 1900s, there were continuous Mexican revolutions, political upheavals, and violent raids. The names of Poncho Villa, Venustino Carranza, and Emiliano Zapata created fear in the northern villages, where soldiers raped and kidnapped young girls and forced young boys at gunpoint to join the revolutionary armies. Mexicans were streaming into San Antonio to escape the bloodshed, poverty, and lack of jobs. Between 1910 and 1920, more than 25,000 Mexicans made their way across the border by train, by car, by wagon, and even by walking or swimming across the Rio Grande River. The rapid exodus brought many social problems, such as lack of housing and opportunities for employment, to the West Side of the city, where most of the Mexican immigrants settled.

There was also a great need for schools and churches. The Catholic Bishop, John W. Shaw, encouraged the Claretian missionaries to construct a new church in the area. Under the energetic leadership of Father Ramon Prat, they began their work on the West Side of San Antonio with the construction in 1912 of Immaculate Heart of Mary Church. Later, the missionaries built a convent and school, and organized the Society of Christ the King, the Guadalupanas, and other groups to serve the parish members. In the first fifty years of the parish, there were 35,727 baptisms, 4,232 marriages, and 14,948 confirmations.

In 1942, the church needed refurbishing and a man whose identity has been lost, was commissioned by the Claretians to redo the interior. The artist had painted the interior of *Nuestra Senora Reyna de Los Angeles* Church in California, and the quality and the beauty of his work was widely recognized. He used stencils to paint designs on the ceiling of Immaculate Heart of Mary Church, but unfortunately his work deteriorated with time.

In 1985, Father Alberto Domingo began restoring the church again. The Cuban-born priest had great artistic talent and became recognized as the church's Michelangelo. He had a lifelong fear of heights, but was determined to re-paint the ceiling. "I made a deal with Our Lady," the priest said. "I told her, 'You take this fear of heights from me and I will rebuild your church.' " The work demanded that he stand on a thirty-foot-high scaffold to paint the ceiling and to endure not only his fear of heights but also the Texas heat in the high, enclosed space. He also restored several statues and the Stations of the Cross.

After working six years, Father Domingo was transferred. His work was not finished, and a search began for another painter. Father Joseph Gamm asked Pedro Briones, who was painting the gutters of the church, to do the job. Briones refused to take on the task which he felt would be too difficult. When Father Gamm informed him, however, that after the gutters were finished, there would be no more work for him to do, the painter quickly changed his mind. To assist him in his work, Father Gamm drove to a day labor area on West Commerce Street and picked a strong-looking man named Jose Valdez. Briones and Valdez formed a marvelous team, and working together they painted the ceiling by hand.

In 1991, they had nearly completed the majestic repainting when a fire that seemed to have been deliberately set, broke out in the building. The paint decorations on the vault over the altar were almost totally destroyed and much of the interior was smoke-damaged. Briones and Valdez, however, went back to work and meticulously created an astonishing artistic masterpiece for the church.

Over time, highway construction and urban renewal have greatly reduced the number of parishioners at Immaculate Heart of Mary Church. Nevertheless, there is a great loyalty to this parish which has produced a large number of priestly and religious vocations. The Claretian congregation continues to serve the parish with great enthusiasm for its community in downtown San Antonio.

DESIGN–ARCHITECTURE

The church was designed in Romanesque revival style by Leo M. J. Dielmann, a renowned and prolific architect who was responsible for the magnificent chapel at Our Lady of the Lake University and many other buildings in San Antonio. The façade is in two tones of light and dark tan brick with limestone accents and a maroon colored standing-seam tin roof and gutters. Dielmann's father, J. C. Dielmann, was the contractor for the building.

The façade has three arched doors. Above the center door is a rose window and a bell tower with a steeple and a cross. The north and south sides of the church each contain three brick bastion-like appendages, two of which are later additions that provide space for side altars and confessionals. The higher parts of the exterior walls, as well as the windows, are constructed with round Romanesque arches. Statues of Our Lady of Guadalupe, St. Juan Diego, and Christ the King have been added to the exterior of the church.

Many different colors, especially bright blue, have been used for the interior ceilings and walls that were originally painted white. An array of quatrefoil motifs which have a Moorish design cover the entire ceiling. There are colorful stained glass windows, some of which came from the Polish church, St. Michael's, that was demolished in preparation for the 1968 Hemisfair in San Antonio. The sanctuary has original work done by Father Alberto Domingo depicting the four evangelists in faux mosaic.

Statues of St. Anthony Claret, founder of the Claretian congregation, and of the Immaculate Heart of Mary adorn the interior of the church. The crown of the Immaculate Heart of Mary statue is said to have been made from jewels and gold donated by the parishioners. The dome above the statue is outlined with Tivoli lights and has ribs that spring from *trompe l'oeil* brackets. There are six side altars and an attractive set of the Stations of the Cross. The church is a masterpiece of decorative painting and stained glass.

INTERESTING STORIES

A very special and rich piece of Texas history revolves around the bell of San Fernando Church that was used to announce the fall of the Alamo. Supposedly, the same bell tolled for hours for the burial of the remains of the great Texas heros, William Barrett Travis, Davy Crocket, and James Bowie in the sanctuary of San Fernando Church. In 1904, when a new set of four bells was purchased for the twin towers of the cathedral, the old bell from San Fernando Church that had been rung at the fall of the Alamo was somehow lost and a mystery developed over its disappearance. Where did this bell go? Many years later in 1927, Father Leo Monasterio, a Claretian missionary from Mexico, explained the mystery in his writings. Father Monastero claimed the old bell had been installed in the bell tower of Immaculate Heart of Mary Church shortly after its completion in 1912. It is believed that the treasured bell still rings at the church thus connecting the parish to the history of the Alamo.

In 1914, religious persecution broke out in Mexico, and many bishops, priests, and sisters fled to San Antonio for protection. The Immaculate Heart of Mary Church's residence became a place of safety for more than 108 priests, including members of the Catholic hierarchy who were received and sheltered by the Claretians.

SAN FRANCESCO
DI PAOLA CHURCH

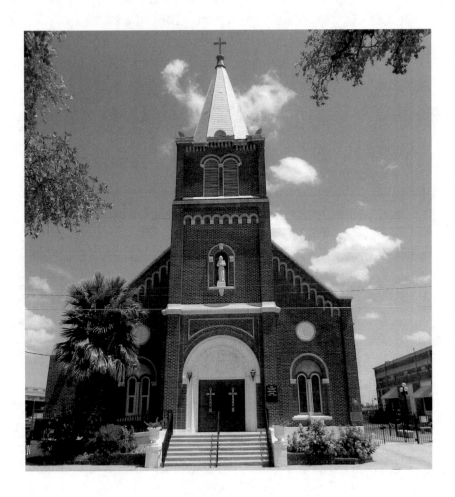

LOCATION

San Francesco di Paola Church is located on Piazza Italia, north of W. Martin Street between N. Santa Rosa Street and Interstate 35. It faces Columbus Park and is just north of the CHRISTUS Santa Rosa Hospital Complex.

MISSION

The Catholic community of San Francesco di Paola has chosen as its misson to grow in the love and knowledge of God the Father, Son, and Holy Spirit through the celebration of Mass, the sacraments, the study of scripture, and the sharing of mutual talents. The congregation strives to build the body of Christ and to help the needy, with special emphasis on Italian culture and customs.

HISTORY

In March, 1926, Father Saverio Vecchio came to San Antonio to escape the violent persecution directed toward religious communities in Mexico. Upon his arrival, the energetic forty-eight-year-old Italian priest put together a weeklong mission at San Fernando Cathedral for the Italian community of the city. A highly successful revival stirred the religious and patriotic devotion of many of the Italian immigrants and gave rise to the idea of building a church for their community. Initially, a local hall was used for worship so the community would have a place where the people could listen to the homily of the Mass in Italian. This experience was deeply moving for many persons in the growing Italian community since it was the first time many of them had heard the homily as well as parts of the Mass in their native language.

A fever of enthusiasm and generosity caught hold, and soon construction began on a new church which the people decided to name San Francesco di Paola after the much-loved fifteenth-century Italian saint, known throughout rural communities in southern Italy. The structure was completed in less than a year.

In May, 1927, the new church was blessed, followed by great festivities that included dancing, entertainment, and musical programs in Franklin Park, now Columbus Park, in front of the church. There were traditional Italian costumes and food booths for the families as they gathered to dedicate their church. Archbishop Arthur J. Drossaerts, ten priests, and the Knights of Columbus were present for the occasion. After the opening Mass, there was a banquet with more food, drink, singing, and dancing that lasted till midnight. The celebration is remembered to this day by the Italian congregation.

After fifteen years of faithfully paying off the loan of $39,839 for the cost of their church, the congregation had one final drive to raise the remaining $8,080. When they accomplished their goal, they had a "burning of the mortgage" celebration on May 7, 1944, that included a solemn High Mass of Thanksgiving, the actual burning of the mortgage document, spaghetti and meatball dinner, cake, coffee, and dancing. San Francesco di Paola still stands proudly because of the efforts of so many within San Antonio's Italian community who are deeply committed to this small but extraordinary church.

Design–Architecture

The architect for San Francesco di Paola was Richard Vander Stratten, who was also known in San Antonio for helping to design the once swank Aurora Apartments built in the 1930s. Vincent Falbo and Louis Guido were the general contractors.

The church holds 300 people. It is Romanesque in design and was built with red brick and contrasting white brick trim. A white niche with the statue of San Francesco di Paola is located above the double doors that have two large gold crosses as well as carvings of grapevines and the crown of thorns. Many arches in white brick adorn the church, as well as a white steeple with a large gold cross. On the left side of the church is a brick addition in a rounded shape that houses a special statue of Mary, the Mother of Jesus.

Next to the San Francesco di Paola Church is Columbus Hall, which is used for receptions, events, and the congregation's popular spaghetti dinners. Between the buildings is a garden with a large statue of San Francesco which came from Rome and a statue of Our Lady of Guadalupe. This is a quiet area for prayer and peace.

The main doors of San Francesco di Paola open to a small foyer with several marble plaques lining both sides of the walls in honor of deceased members of the congregation. Another set of doors opens to the sanctuary with two beautiful, large, white marble angels holding shells containing holy water. On the right near the entry is a prayer area with candles and statues of St. Cosmas and St. Damian, who were twins and physicians. The statues were given to the church by Santa Rosa Hospital. The Stations of the Cross are indentified in Italian titles. There is also a picture of the Madonna Della Sfida, the universal patron of policemen and fire-fighters that San Francesco di Paola is honored to display since it is the only copy of the painting in the United States. The original is in the Cathedral of Barletta near Rome.

Behind the main altar is a large, impressive statue of San Francesco Di Paola, the patron saint of the Italian community.

Throughout the church, combinations of white marble and shades of green are found on the eight faux marble columns. The church has a terrazzo floor and wooden trim. Beneath the statue of San Francesco is a tabernacle made of gold and copper. There are two side altars, two large shelves in the form of flowers that hold statues of Jesus and St. Jude. All the marble and most of the statues were brought from Italy and were donated by various parishioners whose names are found underneath. There are many stained-glass windows and chandeliers trimmed with glittering crystals. The church contains also a rounded shrine housing a statue of the Sorrowful Mother. The wooden pews have cap snaps providing a place for gentlemen to hang their hats.

Of special interest are the relics in this church. In Christianity, relics are the material remains of a deceased saint or martyr as well as objects closely associated with those remains. Until 1969, Roman Catholics usually placed relics in the altars of their churches. In San Francesco di Paola Church, the main altar contains a relic of St. Severiani, martyr, while the right side altar has gold reliquaries which hold relics of San Francesco di Paola and St. Philip Neri.

INTERESTING STORY

San Francesco di Paola was a saint who was especially loved by the people of Spezzano, a village in southern Italy. He particularly looked after the poor by always supporting them and performing many miracles on their behalf. At one time, he cured a young man's arm wound with a common herb. When asked how he did this, he replied, "It is faith that works miracles."

San Francesco was a vegetarian, since his love of animals prevented him from killing them for consumption. He had a vast garden which he was said to have shared with the poor of his village. Each September, the rural community continues to hold a procession in his memory and in celebration of the growth of successful crops.

The custom is continued at the Church of San Francesco di Paola in San Antonio. Each September, the church offers a Mass in thanksgiving for fall crops. Church members greet congregants at the door with prayer cards and fresh flowers. Near the altar, the statue of San Francesco di Paola is draped with a satin ribbon around the shoulders on which many people pin donations that will be used to help feed the hungry in San Antonio. The readings for the Mass are offered in Italian and English. At the end of the service, the people process outside, and the statue of San Francesco di Paola is carried on a wooden platform around Columbus Park. Special prayers are recited during the ceremony and later, children dressed in native costumes perform traditional Italian folk dances.

APPENDICES

MAP OF DOWNTOWN SAN ANTONIO

The location of the various churches and chapels discussed in the book are indicated by numbers referring to the list that follows.

1. The Alamo
2. San Fernando Cathedral
3. *La Capilla de los Milagros*
4. First Presbyterian Church
5. Ursuline Academy and Chapel
6. Travis Park United Methodist Church
7. St. John's Lutheran Church
8. St. Mary's Catholic Church
9. St. Mark's Episcopal Church
10. First Baptist Church
11. St. Joseph's Catholic Church
12. Little Church of La Villita
13. Madison Square Presbyterian Church
14. Central Christian Church
15. Grace Lutheran Church
16. Immaculate Heart of Mary Catholic Church
17. San Francesco di Paola Catholic Church

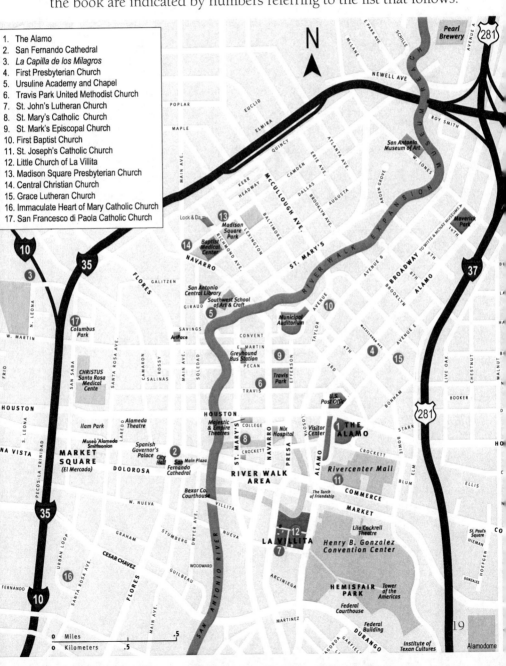

LOCATIONS AND GENERAL INFORMATION

1. THE ALAMO

300 Alamo Plaza
San Antonio, Texas 78299
(210) 225-1398

Mailing address:
P.O. Box 2599
San Antonio, Texas 78205

Open daily, except Christmas Eve and Christmas Day
Hours: 9:00a.m.-5:30p.m., Monday-Friday
10:00a.m.-5:30p.m., Saturday-Sunday
Open until 7:00p.m. June, July, and August

The reenactment of the Battle of the Alamo is staged on March 6.

2. SAN FERNANDO CATHEDRAL

115 Main Plaza
San Antonio, Texas 78205
(210) 227-1297

Masses:
Saturday 8:00 a.m., 5:30 p.m.
Sunday 6:00 a.m., 8:00 a.m. (televised on channel 15 and 41),
    10:00 a.m., 12 noon, 2:00 p.m., 5:00 p.m.
Monday-Friday 12:05 p.m.
Tuesday-Friday 6:15 a.m.

Reenactment of the Crucifixion of Jesus Christ is held on
    Good Friday in front of the cathedral.

3. LA CAPILLA DE LOS MILAGROS

113 Ruiz Street
San Antonio, Texas 78205

Open daily, except Tuesday, 9:00 a.m.-2:00 p.m.

4. First Presbyterian Church

404 North Alamo Street
San Antonio, Texas 78205
(210) 226-0215

Sunday services: 9:00 a.m., 10:00 a.m., 11:00 a.m., 11:15 a.m.

Open to visitors by request Monday-Friday 8:30 a.m.-5.00 p.m.

5. Ursuline Academy and Chapel

300 Augusta Street
San Antonio, Texas 78205
(210) 224-1848

Open Monday-Saturday 10:00 a.m.-5:00 p.m.
Sunday 11:00 a.m.-4:00 p.m.
Docent Tours: daily 11:00 a.m.

Fiesta Art Fair is held in April during Fiesta Week.

6. Travis Park United Methodist Church

230 East Travis Street
San Antonio, Texas 78205
(210) 226 - 8341

Sunday services: 9:30 a.m., 11:00 a.m.

Open to visitors by request Monday-Friday 8:30 a.m.-2:30 p.m.

7. St. John's Lutheran Church

502 East Nueva Street
San Antonio, Texas 78205
(210) 223-2611

Sunday service: 9:30 a.m.

Open to visitors by request Monday-Thursday 8:00 a.m.-4:45 p.m
    Friday 8:00 a.m.-4:00 p.m.
Coronation pageant is held in March. Check with the office for
exact date.

8. St. Mary's Catholic Church
202 North St. Mary's Street
San Antonio, Texas 78205
(210) 226-8381

Open daily from 8:00 a.m.-2:00 p.m.

Daily mass: Monday-Saturday 12:00 noon
Saturday 5:30 p.m.
Sunday 8:00 a.m., 10:00 a.m., 12:00 noon, 6:00 p.m.

9. St. Mark's Episcopal Church
315 East Pecan Street
San Antonio, Texas 78205
(210) 226-2426

Sunday services: 7:45 a.m., 9:00 a.m., 11:15 a.m. September-May
Summer 10:00 a.m.

Open to visitors by request Monday-Friday 8:30 a.m.-5:00 p.m.

Free concerts, "Music from St. Mark's," on Sundays at 4.00 p.m.
Call for dates.

10. The First Baptist Church of San Antonio
515 McCullough Avenue
San Antonio, Texas 78215
(210) 226 - 0363

Sunday services: 9:15 a.m., 11:00 a.m. (Televised KSAT 12, Cable 13)

Open to visitors by request Monday-Friday 8:30 a.m.-5:00 p.m.

Special Ministry: 4th Street Café offers home-style cooking to the
general public with proceeds donated to the homeless. Open
Monday-Friday from 11.00 a.m.-1:00 p.m.

11. St. Joseph's Catholic Church
623 E. Commerce St.
San Antonio, Texas 78205
(210) 227-0126

Church is open daily 8:00 a.m.-4:00 p.m.

Masses:
Sunday: 8:00 a.m., 9:30 a.m., 11:00 a.m., 12:30 p.m.
Monday-Friday 12:00 noon
Saturday: 12 noon, 5:00 p.m.

The Liederkranz Choir sings every fourth Sunday in German and
English at the 11:00 a.m. Mass.

12. LITTLE CHURCH OF LA VILLITA
418 Villita Bldg. 1300
San Antonio, Texas 78205
(210) 226-3593

Services:
Thursday and Sunday 11:00 a.m.

Open daily to visitors 10:00 a.m.-5:30 p.m.

Starving Artist Art Show is held the first weekend in April at
La Villita Arts Village.

13. MADISON SQUARE PRESBYTERIAN CHURCH
319 Camden Street
San Antonio, Texas 78215
(210) 226-6254

Sunday service: 10:50 a.m.

Open to visitors by request Monday-Thursday 9:00 a.m.-4 p.m.
Friday 9:00 a.m.-12 noon

14. CENTRAL CHRISTIAN CHURCH
720 N. Main Avenue
San Antonio, Texas 78205
(210) 227-5273

Sunday service: 10:55 a.m. Open to visitors by request Monday
Friday 8:30 p.m.-4:00 p.m.

The carillon is played each Sunday after the service.

15. GRACE LUTHERAN CHURCH
504 Avenue E
San Antonio, Texas 78215
(210) 226-9131

Sunday service: 10:30 a.m.

Open to visitors by request Monday-Thursday 8:00 a.m.-4 p.m.
    Friday 8 a.m.-noon

Easter Sunrise Service is held at the Arneson Theatre.

16. IMMACULATE HEART OF MARY CATHOLIC CHURCH
517 South Santa Rosa Avenue
San Antonio, Texas 78204
(210) 226-8268

Masses:
Sunday 9:00 a.m., 10:30 a.m., 12:00 noon, 5:00 p.m
Saturday 8:00 a.m., 5:30 p.m.

Open to visitors by request Monday-Friday 9:00 a.m.-1:00 p.m.,
    and 2p.m.-5:30 p.m. (Enter through the rectory side door.)

17. SAN FRANCESCO DI PAOLA CATHOLIC CHURCH
205 Piazza Italia
San Antonio, Texas 78207
(210) 227-0548

Masses:
Sunday 10:00 a.m.
Tuesday - Friday 12:00 noon
Saturday 5:30 p.m.

Open to visitors by request Tuesday-Friday 9 a.m. - 2 p.m.

Spaghetti dinners are held four times a year. Call rectory for exact
    dates.

Fall Procession in honor of San Francesco di Paola. Call rectory
    for exact date.

SOURCES OF INFORMATION AND SELECTED REFERENCES

Allen, Stewart and Phyllis. Personal Interview. 6 September 2011.

Aniol, Betty Sue. *To God Alone the Glory, the History of St John's Lutheran Church*. San Antonio: Historical Publishing Network, 2007.

Brevard, Rosemary. Personal Interview. 10 March 2012.

Davis, Rev. Bill, OMI. Telephone Interview. 1 April 2011.

Dennis, Doran. Personal Interview. 10 February 2012.

Edwards, Emily. *F. Giraud and San Antonio*. San Antonio: The Southwest Craft Center, 1985.

—. *Stones, Bells, Lighted Candles*. San Antonio: Daughters of the Republic of Texas, 1981.

Elizondo, Rev. Virgilio and Timothy M. Matovina. *San Fernando Soul of the City*. New York: Orbis Press, 1998.

Elizondo, Rev. Virgilio. Personal Interview. 5 April, 2012.

Everett, Donald E. *Adobe Walls to Stone Edifice*. Austin: Best Printing Company, 1995.

Ferruzzi, Gloria. Personal Interview. 4 April 2010.

Fisher, Lewis F. *Saint Mark's Episcopal Church*. San Antonio: Maverick Publishing Company, 2008.

Fitzhugh, Forrest. E-mail to the author. 15 April 2012.

Furey, Most Rev. Francis J. *Archdiocese of San Antonio 1874-1974*. San Antonio: Archdiocese of San Antonio, 1974.

Garcia, Rev. David. Telephone Interview. 11 March 2012.

Greco, Sam. Personal Interview. 14 April 2012.

Gottschalk, Paul. Personal Interview. 8 November 2010.

Greer, Bob. Personal Interview. 20 March 2011.

Groneman, Bill. *Alamo Defenders a Genealogy: The People and Their Words*. Austin: Eakin Press, 1990.

Habig, Marion A. *The Alamo Chain of Missions*. Chicago: Franciscan Herald Press, 2004.

Hatley, Mr. and Mrs. Roy. *A Ninety-Year Record of Madison Square Presbyterian Church*. San Antonio: Munguia Printing Company, 1972.

In the Shadow of his Hand, The First Century of the First Baptist Church of San Antonio, Texas, 1861-1961. San Antonio: Percy Printing Company, 1961.

Johnson, Craig. *A Century of Grace*. San Antonio: Clark (Cenveo), 2003.

—. Personal Interview. 21 April 2010.

Kearney, Milo and Francis Galan. *San Antonio's Churches*. Charleston, South Carolina: Acadia Publishing, 2012.

Kutchins, Kay. Personal Interview. 26 April 2012.

Landregan, Steve. *Catholic Texans Our Family Album*. Strasburg: *Editions du Signe*, 2003.

Loch, Edward, SM. Personal Interviews. 2010-2012.

Mann, Collen McCalla. *So We Can Proceed: A History of Central Christian Church in San Antonio, Texas, 1883-1976*. San Antonio: Central Christian Church, 1978.

Miller, Ray. *Eyes of Texas Travel Guide*. Houston: Cordovan Corporation Publishers, 1979.

Montague, Rev. George, SM. Personal Interview. 10 October 2010.

Nelson, George. *The Alamo an Illustrated History.* San Antonio: Aldine Press, 2009.

Noonan, Mary Ann. *The Missions of San Antonio.* San Antonio: The Alamo Press, 1982.

Nordan Memorial Carillon 50th Anniversary Celebration. San Antonio: n.p., 1953.

Pantuso, Frank. Personal Interview. 18 September 2011.

Pfeiffer, Maria Watson. *School by the River 1851–2001.* San Antonio: Maverick Publishing Company, 2001.

Reyes, Alice. Personal Interview. 1 July 2011.

Rybczyk, Mark Louis. *San Antonio Uncovered.* Plano, Texas: Wordware Publishing, Inc.,1992.

Slattery, Margaret Patrice, CCVI. *Promises To Keep: A History of the Sisters of Charity of the Incarnate Word, Volume One.* San Antonio: Sisters of Charity of the Incarnate Word, 1995.

Steinfeldt, Cecilia. *San Antonio Was: Seen Through a Magic Lantern.* San Antonio: San Antonio Museum Association, 1979.

Steubben, Rev. Lawrence J. Personal Interview. 12 March 2010.

Suttle, Brother Richard, CMF. Personal Interview. 9 May 2012.

We Finish to Begin: A History of Travis Park United Methodist Church, San Antonio, Texas, 1846-1991. San Antonio: Travis Park United Methodist Church, 1991.

White, Kristin E. *A Guide to the Saints.* New York: Ballantine Books, 1991.

Wood, Robert D., SM. *John Twohig An Extraordinary Irish Immigrant.* San Antonio: Pecan Grove Press, 2009.

PHOTO CREDITS

Courtesy of Sean Graham p.9

Courtesy of Father Alberto Borruel p.22

Courtesy of Archdiocese of San Antonio Archives p.37

Courtesy of Stewart Allen p.44

Courtesy of James D. Ludwick LN pp.42, 49

Courtesy of St. Philip's College Archives p.83

Courtesy of Doran Dennis p.97

ABOUT THE AUTHOR

Mary Jane Hardy, a native San Antonio, is a lifelong educator and holds both a bachelor's and a master's degree from The University of the Incarnate Word. Her religious faith has been a source of strength throughout her life, and combined with the support and encouragement of her late husband, Ken Hardy, has served as an inspiration in writing this book.